HEXHAM HER

Tom Corfe

Hexham Civic Society
1999

The first version of *Hexham Heritage* appeared in 1991. This book has the same purpose: to explain how and why Hexham became the town it is, and to introduce its rich heritage to those living in the town and those visiting it. It owes much to the help of many friends over several years, including Stan Beckensall, Eric Cambridge, Colin and Marjorie Dallison, Flora Fairbairn and Janet Goodridge of Tynedale Museums, Brian Jenkins, Anna Rossiter, Peter Ryder, Austin Willson; and to my wife Sheila. It owes much to everyone else who has written about the history of Hexham; some of their works are listed in the note on page 58.

St Wilfrid, on the previous page, is from the drawing by C C Hodges of the 15th-century painting in the Abbey.

Like all country towns, Hexham had many rural industries, often concerned with the hides, skins and fleeces of cattle, sheep and goats. Tanneries lined the banks of the Cockshaw Burn, where the names of pubs and streets still recall the industry. This drawing is based on one from about 1810. Hides are lifted from a lime-pit where they have soaked for days, scraped and 'bated' in solutions of dog excrement and ground bark before hanging up to dry. Skinning and glovemaking were among the other local industries; see page 58.

Published by Tom Corfe, 20 Hudshaw Gardens, Hexham NE46 1HY (01434) 603562 for Hexham Civic Society, and printed by the Abbey Press, Commercial Place, Priestpopple, Hexham NE46 1PG.

©Tom Corfe 1999

ISBN 0 9517996 1 4

1. BEGINNINGS

Hexham is a country town with a rich heritage, the market and administrative centre for Tynedale. For centuries it stood close to the troubled front line of English history, and long before that it played a key part in the vanguard of European Christianity.

Hexham lies near the head of the Tyne, where the North Tyne from Kielder and the Scots border meets the South Tyne flowing from the Cumbrian Pennines, and the united river sets off towards the North Sea. A mile below the confluence Hexham stands on a glacial terrace overlooking the riverside haugh, in a broad green valley flanked by wooded slopes. To the north and south is open farming country, with the moors beyond that rising westwards to the Pennines. Tynedale thrusts into the Pennines and forms the eastern end of the main way across northern England that links the North Sea with the Irish Sea. Travellers have always made use of this route, on foot or on horseback, by road and rail, in the cars, coaches and lorries speeding along the A69. The Romans built the first east-west road along the north side of the valley, later known as the Stanegate. It marked the effective northern limit of their empire, and soon it was given the formidable protection of Hadrian's Wall. So Tynedale became a frontier zone, and it remained one for most of the next fifteen hundred years.

At Corbridge, the Stanegate crossed the Roman road into Scotland, which Anglo-Saxons called the Yorkshiremen's Road (or Dere Street) and the Twentieth Century labelled A68. So from Hexham men might travel with ease eastward or westward; they could go north by Dere Street, or north-west by way of North Tynedale into Scotland, or north-east to the sea and the small ports on the Aln, Coquet and Wansbeck; or they might head south-east towards Durham and Yorkshire. Only the direct way south was blocked by the bare moorlands rising to the highland of western Durham. Many travellers came by many roads to meet at Hexham. They came to trade, to worship or to seek justice; sometimes they came on missions of war.

The documented story of Hexham begins about the year 671, when Queen Æthelthryth (or Etheldreda) of Northumbria gave enough land to Bishop Wilfrid of York to sustain a Christian monastery, and Wilfrid built a great church where the Abbey now stands. We know that people lived in Tynedale long before that: there were hunters before 7000BC, then Neolithic farmers, and Bronze Age folk who left their burial mounds and cists. Perhaps 2500 years ago Iron Age people built defended farmsteads, and went on living in them after Rome imposed protection. Some of these peoples must have lived and grown their crops on the terrace by the Tyne; there was an embanked Iron Age enclosure on Windmill Hill, a smaller version of the fort still visible across the river on top of Warden Hill, and the quernstones which womenfolk used to grind their corn sometimes turn up as evidence of settled arable farming.

A Roman army occupied Tynedale soon after 70AD. They built a fort at Corbridge, the former tribal centre where their two great roads crossed, and it became their principal supply base and a considerable town. Three miles away across the river there may have been a temporary camp on the Hexham terrace, as there were camps all over Tynedale

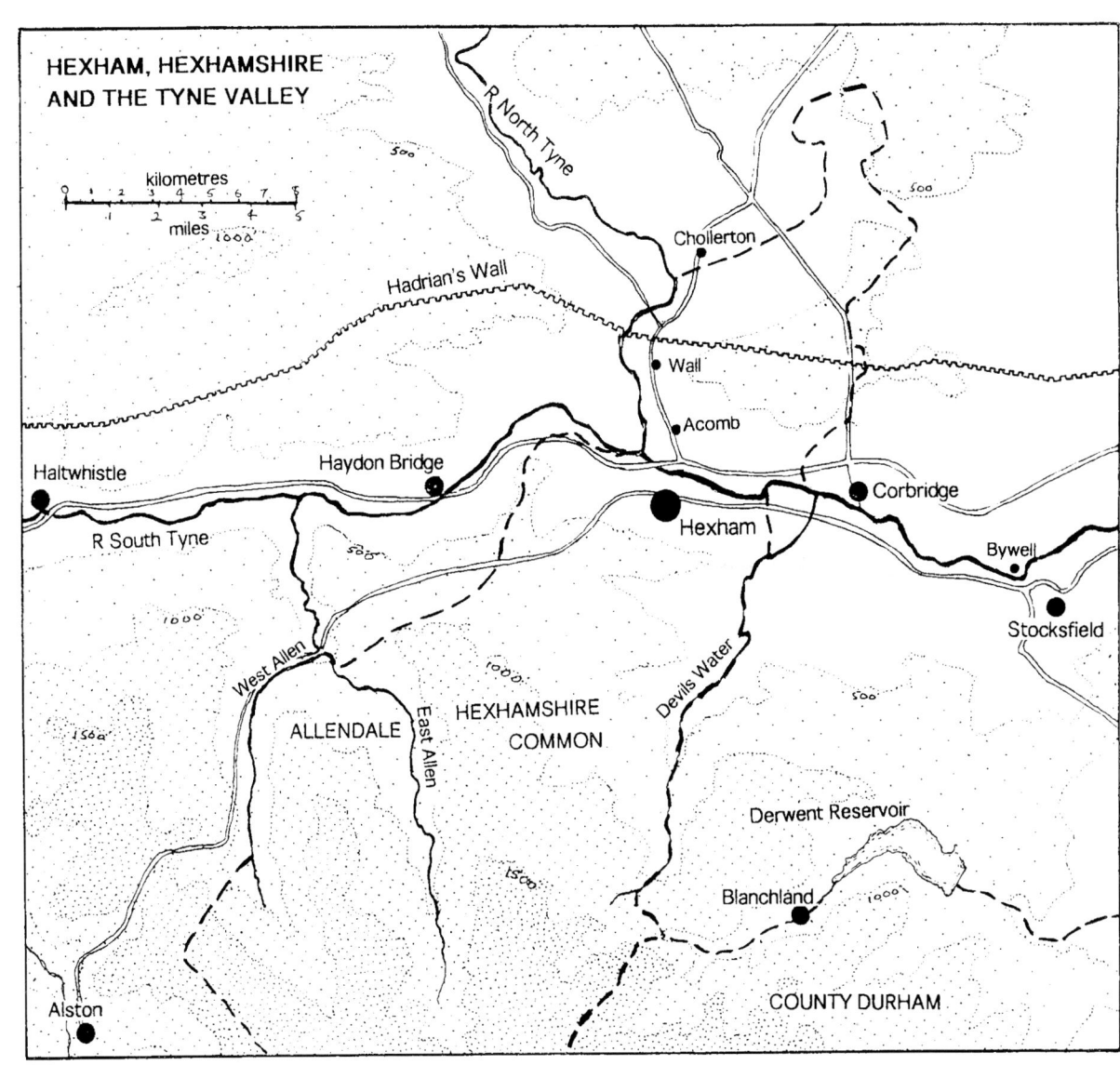

Hexham in its regional setting. The boundary shown is that of Hexhamshire, once the Regality of the Archbishop and perhaps before that the land originally granted to Bishop Wilfrid.

at one time or another during the three centuries of occupation; but there is no trace of anything more permanent such as a stone-built fort or town. Antiquaries and archaeologists have so far failed to find firm evidence in three hundred years of searching. The most that can be said is that the many Roman altars hint at a possible pagan temple somewhere nearby, while the ruins of Roman Corbridge proved invaluable as a quarry for those who built the monastery and the town.

Among the Roman invaders operating around Corbridge was a regiment of auxiliary cavalry from Gaul, the *ala Petriana*. The Petrians had a young standard-bearer named Flavinus, and when he died his colleagues set up in his memory an imposing tombstone that showed him riding in triumph over a cowering enemy. Flavinus, wearing his plumed helmet and carrying a radiate imperial image, can be seen today in Hexham Abbey. His tombstone was found built into later foundations, and originally it may have been brought from the cemetery at Corbridge to serve as building stone.

Roman rule failed about 400AD, leaving local British kings to take over, but of this 'Dark Age' we know almost nothing. It seems likely that Tynedale remained a frontier zone separating rival groups, and it may be that some British or Saxon war-leader set his stronghold on the terrace, where a sharp rise or bluff overlooks the Tyne ford; if so, subsequent building culminating in the present Prospect House has obliterated its traces.

At some time during that Dark Age Tynedale passed from British to Anglo-Saxon domination, from being part of the little-known western kingdom of Rheged to the rising English-controlled Northumbria. The actual transfer may well be linked with dramatic events that took place in Tynedale in or about 634. The Welsh King Cadwallon, champion of Britain for the Britons and of British Christianity, had overrun the Anglo-Saxon North, slaying both the Christian King Edwin and his pagan successor, Eanfrith. Eanfrith's younger brother, Prince Oswald, returned from exile and rallied an army of all who feared Cadwallon's aggression, including Christian Scots and Rheged Britons as well as Northumbrian Anglo-Saxons, who were still mainly pagan. Oswald set up a wooden cross at Heavenfield, beside the Roman Wall, to rally his motley force, and vowed if successful to rule as a Christian. Then he launched a dawn attack on Cadwallon, whose army had been busily ravaging the district from its camp somewhere near the later Whitley Chapel; the Welsh king and his whole army were slain at the Denisesburn, now called the Rowley Burn. The victory ended the last British attempt to recover all Britain, but Christianity was

Flavinus. C C Hodges, the Abbey architect, made this drawing of the Roman memorial soon after he had discovered it in 1881, re-used in later foundations.

preserved because Oswald had chosen to fight as a Christian. Oswald's hosting-place is marked by a modern cross near St Oswald's Church beside the B6318, with a sadly misleading information board alongside it.

Both Heavenfield and the Denisesburn were within a district known soon afterwards as the Hagustald's Land, which may have passed at that very time from Oswald's Rheged allies to Oswald's own younger brother Oswiu. Oswiu was a younger son who inherited no land of his own; if he were granted an estate, he would become what was known as a 'hagustald'. We know that Oswiu married a Rheged princess in or soon after 634, and it seems possible that the marriage cemented the alliance of the two kingdoms, and involved the transfer of an estate. It is likely that the Hagustald's Land became what was later called Hexhamshire.

Oswiu in time succeeded his sainted brother as King of Northumbria, and maintained the Christian faith. But he faced disputes between rival missionaries, those who took their ideas and practices from Ireland, Iona, Rheged and the Celtic fringe, and those who followed the Roman practices brought to Canterbury by St Augustine. In choosing between them Oswiu was swayed by the arguments of a pushful young noble named Wilfrid who spoke up for the Roman cause. Wilfrid had grown up just as Christianity was spreading in Northumbria, and had sampled the Celtic variety by training at the island monastery of Lindisfarne, before setting off on the long journey to Rome. He returned fired with enthusiasm for the splendours of the new faith as practised in Rome and Gaul, and persuaded Oswiu to come down in its favour. Wilfrid was rewarded with the bishopric of York, and he won the favour of Oswiu's daughter-in-law, the pious East Anglian Princess Æthelthryth. Æthelthryth's marriage to Prince Ecgfrith was a political arrangement and a sham; a devout and strong-minded lady, she disliked the rough politics of the Northumbrian court and wished only to retreat to the peace and devotion of the convent. Wilfrid came to her aid, helping her to leave Ecgfrith soon after he had succeeded his father, and to set up her own monastery at Ely. In gratitude she granted to the Bishop the Hagustald's Land, which may have been a wedding portion from her father-in-law.

So Wilfrid built his monastery on the terrace overlooking the Tyne. Perhaps there was already a wooden chieftain's hall on the bluff, and perhaps another on the hill later called the Seal (OE *Sele*=hall). But Wilfrid's monastery and church were intended to put these to shame, for he built in stone to match the splendid churches he had seen on his travels at Rome or during a long stay in Gaul. Anglo-Saxon workmen could manage stout wooden halls, though they had no skill with cold, hard stone; but three miles down the river at Corbridge were vast quantities of the stone that Roman workmen had quarried, shaped and carved to build their fort, cemetery, granaries, town and bridge. So there arose a church that Wilfrid's followers maintained was the finest this side of the Alps, one that far outshone the humble wooden churches of the Celtic missionaries. Its only possible rival was the monastery built at the same time by Wilfrid's friend and fellow-traveller to Rome, Benedict Biscop, on land at Wearmouth given him by King Ecgfrith.

Wilfrid was proud, combative and ambitious. He sought to wield the kind of political influence that he had seen exercised by Gaulish bishops, and this led him into conflict with the Northumbrian king and with the Archbishop of Canterbury. He also wanted his church to be enriched with treasures that would underline its importance and draw all Northumbrians towards the Christian fold. It seems likely that he had made a throne of carved stone, such as he had seen in Gaulish cathedrals, a seat that has survived through all the changes at the Abbey. It is also likely that he brought back from one of his journeys a most precious relic, though that did not survive; in Rome Wilfrid had often prayed at

The Frith Stool. *Drawings by Birtley Aris show the stone seat as it is today, and as it might have appeared when in use as the throne of abbot and bishop.*

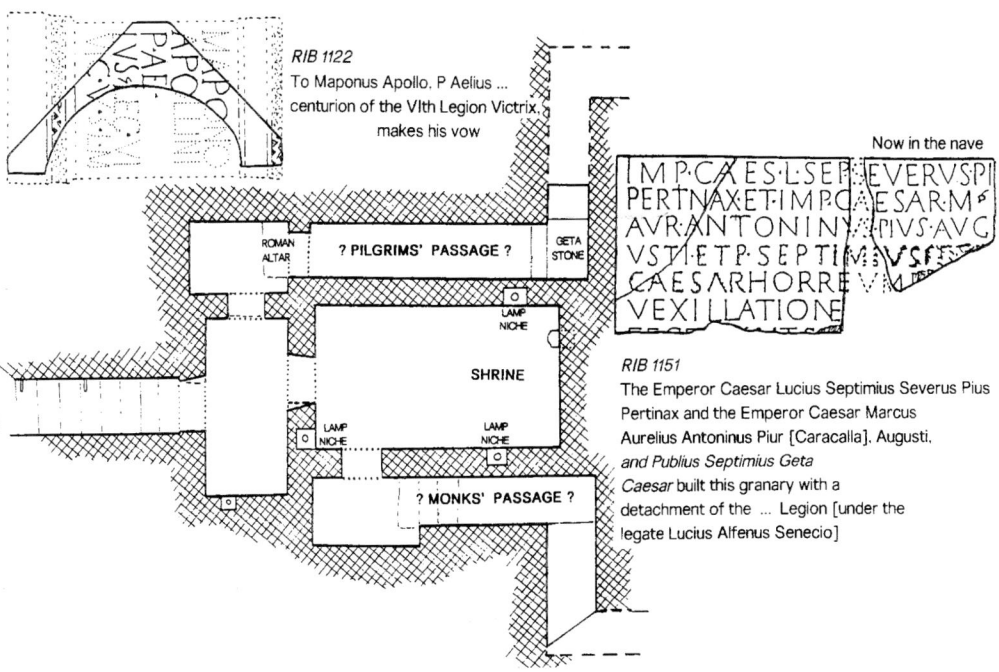

The Crypt. *Once St Wilfrid's dramatic presentation of the relics of St Andrew inspired awe and faith. The contrast of pitchy dark and glowing light, with the colour and sense of mystery, may have passed away; but a visit to this complex of rooms and passages from the earliest days of English Christianity can still thrill and excite.*

the priory of St Andrew, where Augustine of Canterbury had been prior, and he may well have brought from it a cloth sanctified by contact with the saint's remains to take a place of honour in the church which he had dedicated to St Andrew. This link with the very beginnings of Christianity Wilfrid used to attract converts, and he devised a dramatic setting for it. Pilgrims who made their way to wonder at the great stone church and its marvellous relic entered an outer chapel, a porticus, from which a narrow stair descended into darkness. They groped and stumbled along a passage and around sharp corners until they emerged from the darkness of ignorance to find on their left an archway opening into a chamber glowing with light and colour, where the oil lamps illuminated painted biblical scenes on the walls and glinted on a silver plaque mounted upon the casket that held the treasure. They looked, wondered, prayed, and turned to leave by the stair that took them up to Wilfrid's church, where the high altar was directly above the relic. Wilfrid's crypt still keeps its magic. Though the painted plaster has long gone (revealing the re-used Roman stones, some still with carved friezes and inscriptions), the passageways used by pilgrims and monks are blocked, and the lamp niches hold only grubby candles and electric lights, it is still

*The complex interlace patterns of '**Acca's Cross**', though badly worn and weathered during many centuries of abuse and re-use, still demonstrate the technical and artistic skills of the Hexham school of sculpture, as well as inspiration drawn from Mediterranean vine-scroll patterns appearing in manuscript and metalwork. Traditionally, the tall cross was set at the head of St Acca's grave after his death in 740. Many scholars doubt this, but nevertheless date the cross to the middle of the 8th century. This drawing, showing the intricate details of the interlace, was made by W G Collingwood in the 1920s.*

The Changing Shape of St Andrew's

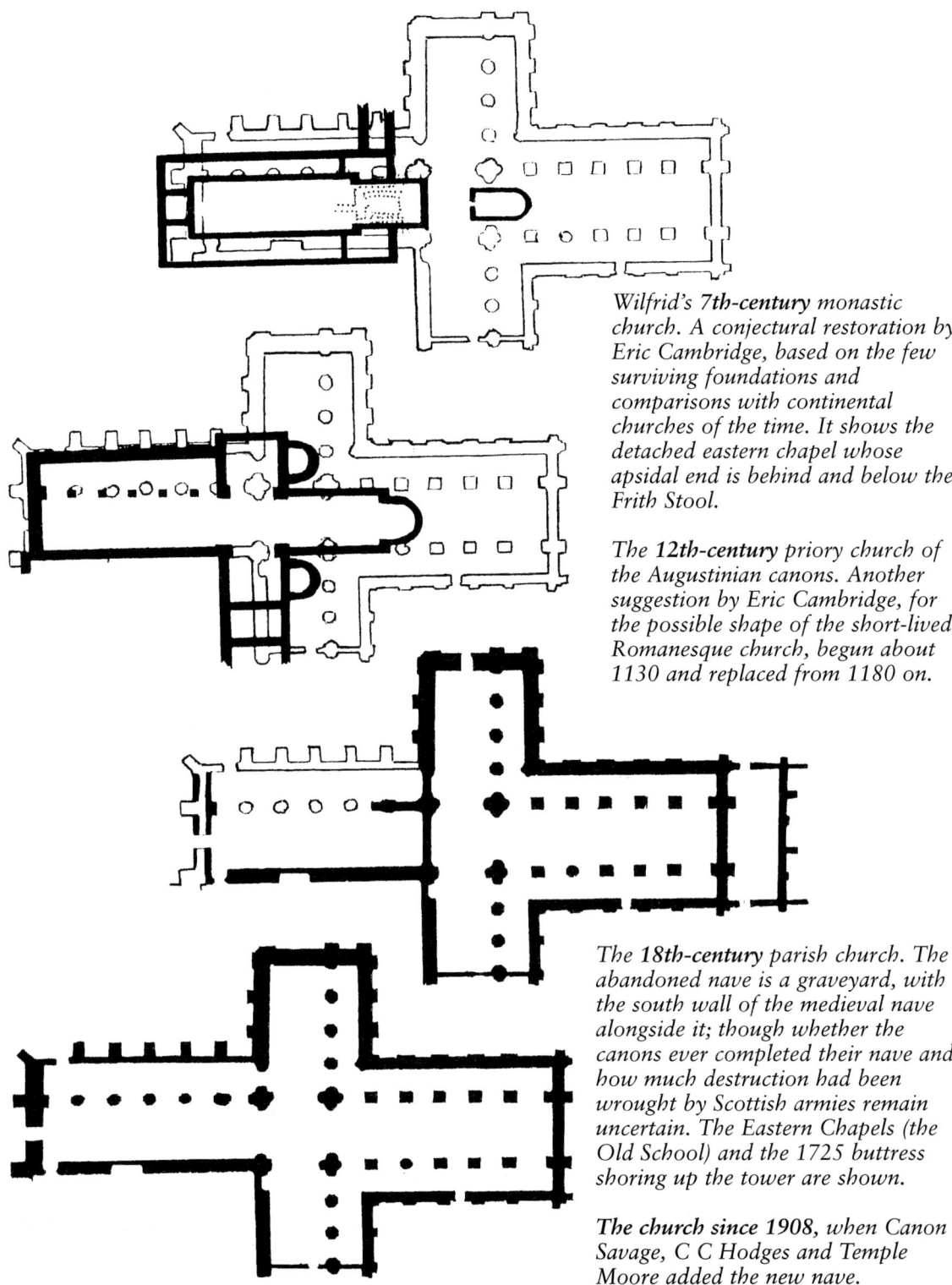

Wilfrid's **7th-century** monastic church. A conjectural restoration by Eric Cambridge, based on the few surviving foundations and comparisons with continental churches of the time. It shows the detached eastern chapel whose apsidal end is behind and below the Frith Stool.

The **12th-century** priory church of the Augustinian canons. Another suggestion by Eric Cambridge, for the possible shape of the short-lived Romanesque church, begun about 1130 and replaced from 1180 on.

The **18th-century** parish church. The abandoned nave is a graveyard, with the south wall of the medieval nave alongside it; though whether the canons ever completed their nave and how much destruction had been wrought by Scottish armies remain uncertain. The Eastern Chapels (the Old School) and the 1725 buttress shoring up the tower are shown.

The church since 1908, when Canon Savage, C C Hodges and Temple Moore added the new nave.

rich with clues to the times of pilgrimage and the showmanship of St Wilfrid.

Of Wilfrid's great church there are many remains, though its shape and size are uncertain. It was long and narrow, with a small chapel beyond its eastern end whose foundations survive below the present chancel. It had winding stairs and passages, and colourful stone friezes; at first the stone came ready carved from Roman Corbridge, but Wilfrid's followers soon learned the stonemason's and sculptor's skills and were able to produce such masterpieces as the cross-shaft linked with Wilfrid's successor, St Acca. Hexham monks were in competition with the heirs to the Celtic tradition at Lindisfarne; if their island monastery could produce the marvellous Lindisfarne Gospels, Hexham could shape proud stone crosses, richly carved and coloured, with elaborate interlace, vine-scrolls and figures.

Wilfrid's monastery became a centre of learning and culture, and played its part in organizing the faith, for from 678 Hexham became the seat of a bishop and Wilfrid's stone seat served as its *cathedra* or bishop's chair. Saintly bishops followed one another in that chair, amongst them Cuthbert (who departed almost at once as he preferred Lindisfarne), John of Beverley, Wilfrid himself when not busy with foreign travel and high politics, and Acca. They appear in the 15th-century paintings in the sanctuary, which may not be from life but are the nearest we can manage to a portrait of Wilfrid.

In time Hexham fell into decline and decay, and it ceased about 821 to serve as a cathedral. Around it, Northumbria was collapsing into a state of chaos and civil war, and there were sea-raiders only too ready to take advantage of its weakness; the Vikings first attacked Lindisfarne in 793. By the 850s the troubles must have reached Hexham, for someone buried all the monastery's small change, about 8,000 coins, in an old bronze bucket. We can only guess at the fate that prevented anyone returning to recover the hoard, for it was only discovered by a gravedigger a thousand years later. Later medieval historians reported that Viking raiders had actually attacked and burned Hexham in 875, for they knew that King Halfdan and a Danish army had camped near the mouth of the Tyne in that year and ravaged northward along the coast; but a Viking visit on that occasion seems unlikely, for Halfdan's stay was short and he soon after met a violent end in Ireland. Whether or not Viking raiders were partly to blame, Wilfrid's great monastery was no more, though an active church continued through the troubled centuries.

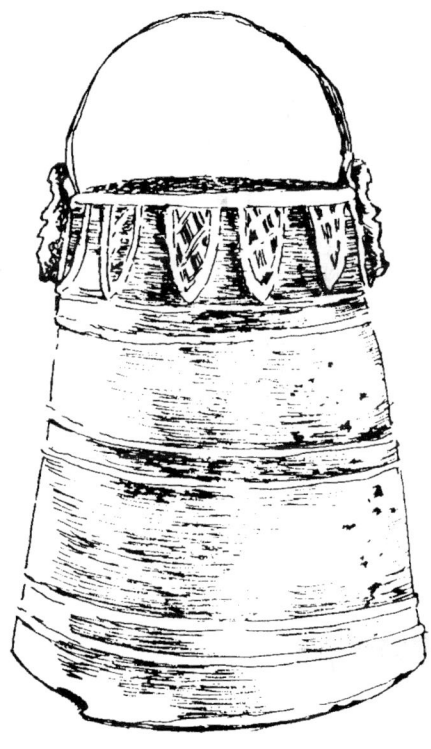

***The Hexham bronze bucket** is now in the British Museum, with a few of the 9th-century coins found in it when it was discovered by a gravedigger in 1832.*

By the 10th century war-torn Northumbria had fallen under the rule of Wessex to become part of the Kingdom of England, but while this change took place a new power grew up in the North. The Bishop of Lindisfarne and his followers had fled from their island church before the Viking threat in 875, carrying with them the remains of their beloved saint, Cuthbert. During the next century, they wandered up and down the north country before settling at Chester-le-Street and then moving in 995 to Durham. During that troubled time men of all ranks often turned to the Community of St Cuthbert for help. When it became necessary to find a new King for York in 883 for example, the Community's influence led to the appointment of a Christian Viking named Guthred. In return grateful lords and rulers (including the ambitious kings of Wessex) gave the Community land and power, and by the time of their move to Durham the Bishop and his followers dominated the north-east of England. It was King Guthred who granted to St Cuthbert's followers the church at Hexham and the former Hagustald's Land that went with it. The Bishop appointed two of his followers from the Community to take charge of these possessions, one as provost (or thane) of the Hagustald's Land and the other as priest of the church. Both were succeeded in time by their sons, and the two families shared the task of running Hexham until the end of the 11th century, when Norman conquerors arrived upon the Northumbrian scene.

St Wilfrid's Gate, *once the main gatehouse of the Priory, has long since lost its upper room and flat roof, although until the early 19th century it retained a vaulted roof and inner passage. It has been tidied and cleaned since this photograph of c1900.*

2. TAKING SHAPE

11th-century Hexham was a small and impoverished community clustered round a half-ruined church; there was but one local smith, and the farming was so poor that the priest had to go hunting to fill the family pot. This at least was the tale told by those who later came to Hexham with a mission to restore faith and hope, the men who woke a decaying settlement to new life.

Northern England passed under new management during the forty years following 1069. The Normans arrived in that year with devastation and massacre, though those who lived north of the Tees escaped lightly compared with the unfortunate folk of Yorkshire. Some of King William's men actually passed through Hexham, but for once Tynedale seems to have avoided the worst. Soon it faced a new threat from north and west, as the Scots of Lothian and Cumbria laid claim to inherited rights over the former Northumbria and the dreaded Malcolm Canmore came to assert his claims with fire and sword. Hexham priests prayed desperately to their saintly predecessors for help, and on at least one occasion Wilfrid and Cuthbert (or some said Acca and Alchmund) obliged by arranging for a dense mist and a flooded river to stop the Scots crossing the Tyne.

The Scots were a recurrent nastiness, but the Normans had come to stay. Warrior lords from northern France imposed the Norman king's authority in every vill and township; there were de Umfravilles at Prudhoe, de Vescis at Alnwick, de Bolbecs at Styford and de Baliols at Bywell. With them came foreign priests and bishops, for Church and Castle worked together to maintain the new order.

Uhtred, Durham's thane of the Hexham lands, deemed it wise to seek Norman protection, and in 1071 submitted to the Norman Archbishop of York. Later in the century Eilaf the priest followed his example by placing the Church of St Andrew in the care of the Archbishop. So Hexham passed from Durham to York. It remained thereafter a fief of the Archbishop and a permanent irritation for the Prince-Bishop of Durham.

Under the Archbishops Hexham enjoyed a new and vigorous life. The Archbishop's possessions stretched for some 22 miles, from Hallington in the north to Allenheads in the south-west, and for some 9 miles across from the West Allen River to the Devil's Water. The Archbishop's Bailiff, who was in charge of all this, had the same sweeping powers as a royal sheriff, for the Archbishop enjoyed the rights within his Regality of Hexham that the King himself held outside it. At the heart of the Regality was St Andrew's Church, and to revive and restore it the Archbishop sent in a team of Augustinian Canons. The canons, product of a religious revival movement that was spreading far and wide from France and Germany, were priests who lived and worked together to maintain and spread the Christian faith. Like monks, they lived by a strict Rule that governed every moment and every action, and regulated prayer and work. Unlike monks, they were active in the wider world rather than seeking seclusion from it, serving in parish church and chapel and among the people. They wore a hooded black cloak over a black cassock and white surplice, they slept in a communal dormitory, and they shared their church with the people of the parish they served, the people of Hexhamshire.

The canons began to arrive in Hexham in 1113, and eventually numbered 26. They set about restoring both the monastic community, ranked now as a priory, and the church that served priory and parish. The rigorous discipline they brought put an end to priestly marriage and slack observance, though the last Eilaf worked alongside the new team until his death in 1138. The canons were devout, energetic and learned, and some were numbered among the greatest scholars of their day; Prior Richard and his successor Prior John wrote best-selling histories, and so did Eilaf's young son, who grew up with the canons before he went off to become the most famous of all Cistercian monks, St Aelred of Rievaulx. The canons encircled their priory with a ten- or twelve-foot wall to separate the religious from the lay community. The precinct wall has all but vanished, save for two short stretches; but it had a profound effect upon the shape of the town that grew outside it. A gatehouse gave access through the wall from Gilesgate, the road along the edge of the terrace that led to the river crossing and the Hospital of St Giles; its roofless lower storey is now known as St Wilfrid's Gate.

Within their new priory wall the canons set to work on rebuilding the church. They wanted to replace the dated and derelict remains of

*The **South Transept** arcades in a dramatic photograph by Stan Beckensall*

the Saxon monastery church with an edifice that reflected Norman confidence, skills and tastes. Their architectural and religious inspiration both came ultimately from France. Their new church would serve both canons and lay worshippers while still keeping them apart; its sturdy round columns and half-round arches would match the splendid nave that was even then nearing completion at Durham. Yet before the masons could complete their new church fashions and minds changed, and if the Romanesque church they planned was ever built, it has left few traces. Instead, their skilled masons began again in the newest Gothic fashion, with richly moulded pointed arches resting on columns of clustered shafts, and a long rectangular choir to replace the curved apse of the Romanesque. Canons at prayer would henceforth face only their brethren beside the high altar, with lay parishioners at their own nave altar beyond the chancel screen. All around their choir and transepts the masons built stately arcades of column, capital and arch; above was a another gallery, the triforium, with two pointed arches inside each semi-circular one, and above that was the clerestory, with tall narrow arches mounted on clustered columns and set in triplets.

The Night Stair led from the canons' dormitory. A series of architectural accidents preserved it. The first 12th-century church was smaller than the later one; the cloister fitted alongside it, and the slype (linking cloister to outer buildings) was immediately south of the transept. When the larger church was built at the end of the 12th century, its transept included the slype, leaving a gallery and a small room above it. So even when the dissolution put an end to the dormitory, the stair still led somewhere, and remained in use. Photograph by Stan Beckensall.

Building work began on the walls and pillars of the chancel about 1175-80, where the choir and sanctuary are the oldest parts of the Augustinian church to survive, though the chancel lost its original easternmost bay when the gable window collapsed in Victorian times. A few years later the south transept was built. Because the canons processed through it eight times daily on their way to service it had to be completed speedily; with no time for elaborate moulding and decoration, the arches are plain and unostentatious. Then came the more ornate north transept with its tall lancet windows, and the crossing that linked these three arms of the church under the massive tower. At long last, it seems, the canons set to work to replace the delapidated and patched Saxon remnant that served as a nave; but we have no idea whether they ever succeeded; there is evidence that at least two starts were made on building a Gothic nave, but only tantalising and inconclusive fragments remain. When the church at length emerged into the light of history and was first pictured in the 17th century, the site of the present nave was a graveyard known as 'Campy Hill' outside its western wall.

One notable piece of church furniture, the venerable bishop's throne, survived from earlier times; placed alongside the high altar, it became the priory's *Frith Stool*, where fugitives might claim sanctuary and the Church's protection. One feature added for the canons ranks with it in interest: the stone stairway down which they nightly found their way from the dormitory for the very first prayers of the day. It is the only intact night stair surviving in Britain.

To support this mighty building effort, and to sustain the canons in the life of prayer and preaching, scholarship and teaching to which they were dedicated, the Archbishop allotted to Hexham Priory widespread estates and smaller properties, with the income from others; and to these lands pious and wealthy laymen added other properties and rent-rolls. Many of the priory holdings were far off, in Yorkshire, Cumbria and Durham; others were closer at hand, such manors as Bingfield, Dotland, Warden, Allerwash, Chollerton. Of most immediate importance were the lands within close range of the priory itself: the vills of Anick and Sandhoe just over the river, and Yarridge, the 'yarrow-grass ridge' to the south. Four holdings lay immediately beyond the precinct wall: in the priory charters they were listed as *Cokeshou*, *Prestpoffel*, *Hennecotes* and *Vicus Fori* (Market Place). In time these small settlements were to be linked as wards of the town that was coming to be known by the name of Hextildesham. Prior Richard and his colleagues might still refer to the 'Hagustaldian Church', but the lay settlements outside the new wall seem to have acquired a new collective name, perhaps taken from the Lady Hextilda, wife of Richard Comyn, who made generous gifts to the priory. Clerks writing the name tended to abbreviate Hextildesham in various ways, but only three centuries later did the town come to be known as Hexham.

Though the priory owned much land on and around the terrace, it did not hold the strong place above the steep eastern bluff. There stood the Bailiff's Hall, made up of a cluster of buildings overlooking the steep 'stile' and the way to the riverside mill and lower ford. Unlike the Priory, the earliest Hall buildings have left no architectural, archaeological or documentary trace; nor did they have such an effect upon the topography of the town. The Hall courtyard had a gatehouse of some sort facing the Priory, where later the Moot Hall replaced it; the buildings were probably enclosed within their own palisade or wall. An imposing hall of timber or stone dominated the group, perhaps on the site of the later Prospect House, and there were smaller buildings for the Bailiff's subordinates: justices, a coroner, the receiver, head forester, sergeant, auditor and gaoler, not to mention workers, craftsmen and their families, an administrative team coping with the economic, legal and social problems of a wide area with a population not much smaller

Medieval Hexham. A reconstruction of the layout of the town in the 14th century.

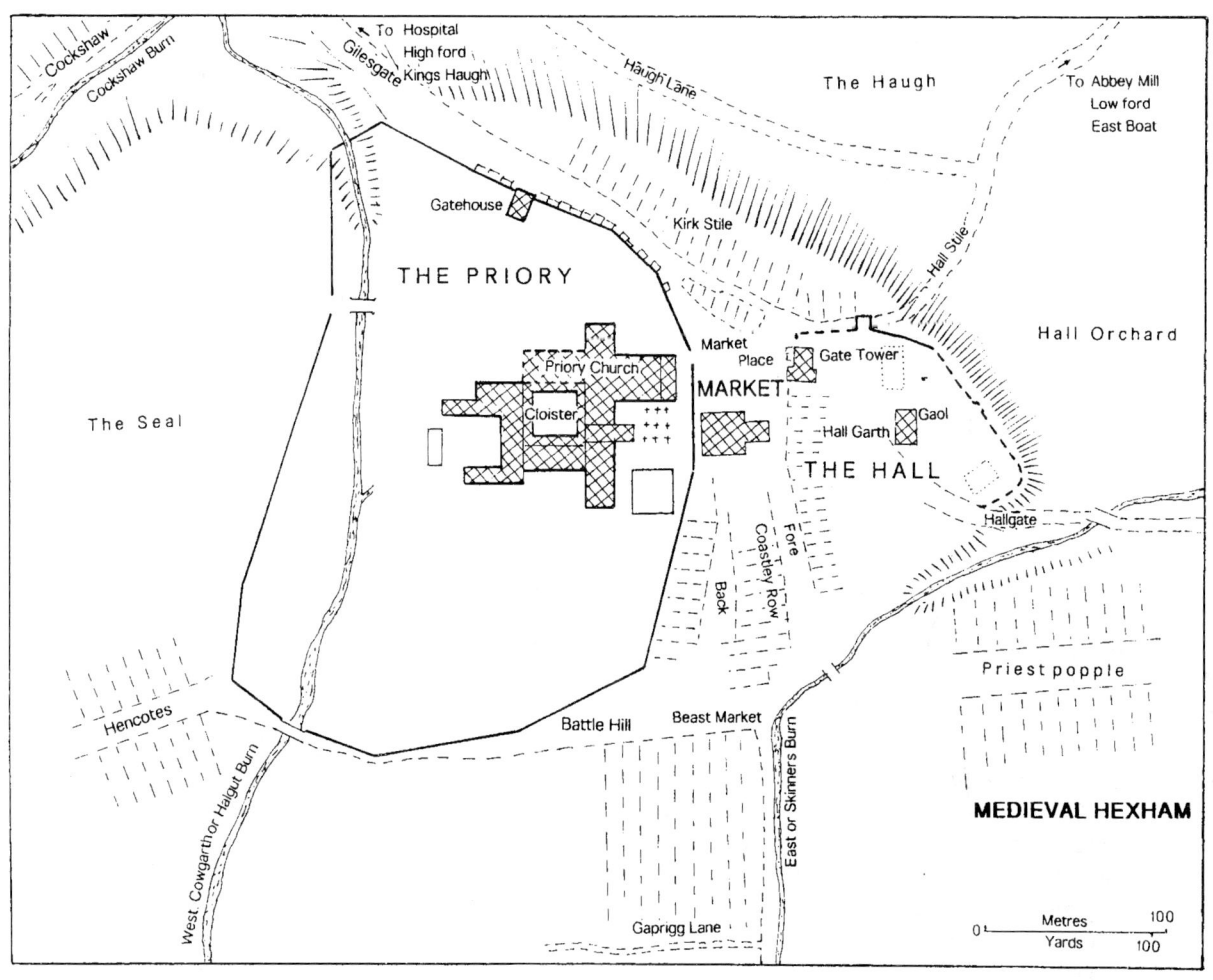

than that of today. The Hall area has remained at the heart of local administration, through the days of Borough Courts, county magistrates, manor office, Urban and Rural District Councils, and the present Tynedale District.

Between the two enclosures lay the Market Place, where it has remained ever since. Some of those who bought and sold in the market lived there also, at first in wooden booths built against the priory wall in what later became Market Street and Back Street. These were rebuilt to become houses and shops, often using recycled stone, once the priory wall had passed out of use. In the middle of the Market Place stood a stone church, the Chapel of St Mary, built by the canons on the site of an earlier church founded by St Wilfrid. Its nave and aisles seem soon to have been occupied by merchants' booths and houses. Other temporary shelters set in the middle of the open spaces to the north and south of the chapel were replaced by permanent houses, to become respectively Market Steads and Coastley Row.

In the century and a half after the coming of the canons, the Priory, the market and the emergent town all flourished. It was a time of peace, and with peace came expansion of trade and arable farming. The many travellers who visited Hexham came to exchange goods or sell produce, or on other peaceful business like an Italian cardinal and his entourage who called in on their way to confer with the King of Scotland in 1151. The violent death of King Malcolm at Alnwick in 1093 ended the worst danger from Scotland, and though his sons kept their claim to Northumbria they reached a compromise by which the Scots king or his son became Earls of Northumberland and held it as vassals of England. Later, they gave up Northumberland to become Lords of Tynedale, which they held until 1290. Neither Northumberland nor Tynedale then included the Regality of Hexham, but the Scots took a close and friendly interest in the Priory and King David I made generous gifts for its support. There was a more warlike visit from David in 1138, when he intervened in the civil wars of Stephen's reign, but he did his best to protect the canons and their church from the unwelcome attentions of his followers. David's ill-fated invasion was a hitch in a mainly peaceful pattern. With a virtual Anglo-Scottish condominium in the North, and effective government in the hands of the Anglo-Norman magnates who served both kings, the Border lost much of its significance. Most great Northumbrian families held lands and titles in Scotland: the Bruces of Hartness and Cleveland held Annandale, the Baliols of Bywell and Barnard Castle held Galloway, and both married great-grand-daughters of King David so both had a claim to the Scottish throne. Gilbert de Umfraville of Prudhoe, who was buried in the Abbey in 1307, was also the Scottish Earl of Angus. Aelred, son of Eilaf the priest, served as one of King David's most active courtiers before turning to religion as a Cistercian. The Lady Hextilda, whose name may appear in Hextildesham, symbolises the mingling of races; her father was Uhtred, the Anglo-Saxon lord of Tynedale, her mother a first cousin of David of Scotland, who gave her in marriage to Richard Comyn, nephew of his Norman chancellor. It was Richard, as Lord of Tynedale under Scots overlordship, who gave valuable landholdings to the Priory of Hexham.

A meeting at York in 1237 of the two kings produced a treaty by which the Scots finally gave up their claims to Northumbria, and agreed to hold their remaining lands south of the Tweed under the English Crown. The fifty years of peace that followed saw Northumbrian agriculture, trade and progress at its peak, and it was a time of maximum growth for the Priory and the settlements that were becoming the town of Hexham. It was in 1239 that Henry lll granted the Archbishop permission to hold a two-day annual fair at Hexham, and a regular Monday market was already established. Sadly, the years of peace came to a sudden end in 1296.

The Hexham Saints. About 1470 the canons of Hexham Priory commissioned these portraits of their saintly precedessors. Third from the left is Wilfrid, shown wearing the pallium of an archbishop, as if the artist sympathised with his thwarted ambitions.
Photograph by Stan Beckensall.

*A **misericord**, in this case showing a bearded and savage Pard, a man-like beast whose mating with a lioness produced the leopard. The carver has enjoyed adding the small figure beside the seat.   Photograph by Stan Beckensall.*

Paintings from the later years of the Priory

The Annunciation

The Passion scenes in the North Choir Aisle show the scourging of Christ before Pilate.

Saints Peter, Andrew and Paul, from Prior Leschman's chapel.

All photographs by Stan Beckensall.

3. TROUBLED TIMES

In 1296 a horde of Scots swept down through North Tynedale and Redesdale, ravaging and burning. When they reached Hexham they set fire to the Priory and much of the town, smashing the holy images and driving out the horrified canons. Rumour had it that they also shut 200 novices in the Priory school, locked the doors and burned them alive. That story, elsewhere told of Corbridge, may be largely English propaganda, but the Scots certainly gave Hexham a shock from which it never really recovered.

Peace on the Scottish Border had become increasingly fragile during the last few years. Edward I of England had been invited to settle Scotland's succession problems when the royal family died out, and gladly obliged, agreeing with the Scots lords that John Baliol of Galloway had a better claim to the crown than Robert Bruce of Annandale. All went well, but then Edward went on to insist that the Scots and their new king accept his rights as overlord of all Britain, and start by helping in his war with France. At this point the Scots and even King John objected, and Edward decided to deal forcibly with them as he had already dealt with the Welsh. Hearing that Edward's army was gathering, the Scots prepared to strike back; a few days after Edward's savage sack of Berwick the Scots surged into Tynedale and burned Hexham.

To some extent Hexham was insulated from Border troubles as a separate regality linked to York, but William Wallace and Robert Bruce were no respecters of such niceties. In 1297 Wallace came, fresh from his triumph over an English army at Stirling Bridge. What was left of the Priory served as his headquarters, and he was gracious enough to grant the surviving canons protection, though his unruly followers treated them and their patron saint with little respect, for Galwegians scorned the Fife-based cult of St Andrew. Fifteen years later Robert Bruce arrived with another army, having finally disposed of his rivals and made himself King of Scotland. For the next ten dreadful years Tynedale was sorely afflicted with Scots; on the few occasions when they did not actually burn and pillage, it was only because they levied crippling blackmail instead; the wealth wrung from Northumberland helped to finance the Scottish triumph at Bannockburn. Even when the Scots were not around, both men and money were needed for the English armies defending the Border and controlling Scotland; the Archbishop constantly demanded recruits and funds to meet royal requirements. Moreover, incessant campaigning, the breakdown of civil order and the widespread misery threw up a riff-raff of violent deserters and homeless adventurers who preyed on law-abiding folk. Such men found the Regality a welcome refuge, for the Archbishop's law-enforcement was even less effective than the King's. As if this were not enough, natural misfortune added to the troubles of Tynedale: there was cattle plague followed by a series of poor harvests, with crops damaged as much by deteriorating weather as by Scottish armies or local brigands. It was reported that many farmers in the Shire had simply abandoned their holdings in despair. The replacement of services and dues in kind by money wages and rents brought new stresses, while in 1349 the spreading disaster of the Black Death added to the misery, as labour was in short supply

Hexham old gaol, as it may have appeared c.1450, from the south-east

The Archbishop's Gaol. A reconstruction by Peter Ryder.

and money even shorter. The result was deepest depression in the countryside and nearly as much misery in the towns.

Harsh conditions produced social friction; workers, farmers and townspeople fell out with one another and with their masters, the Archbishop and the Prior. On occasion both had grudgingly to give up or drastically reduce rents, but this only brought additional ill feeling. In 1330, when peace had for a time been restored with Scotland, the Archbishop wrote with orders for a new prison to be built at Hexham to deal with troublesome tenantry; within two years the new gaol was ready, a fine stone-built square tower equipped with two fearsome dungeons and (at the Archbishop's request) manacles, chains and everything necessary for securing prisoners. Like any substantial building put up in Northumberland during this troubled century, the Gaol Tower was sturdily defensible. Its windows were few and small, and there was a battlemented parapet. The stolid tower has survived later neglect and change of use to remain today as a significant relic of troubled times; it is also the earliest fully documented English prison building.

Some time later this strong tower was joined by another, when the old stone gatehouse of the Hall enclosure was replaced. The new gatehouse tower guarded an entrance tunnel blocked by three pairs of gates; above was a hall with a raised dais where the Bailiff could hold court, and there were living quarters

The Moot Hall, *the Gatehouse to the Bailiff's Hall. Peter Ryder's detailed drawing from* Archaeologia Aeliana 5, XXII (1994) *shows modern door and windows, and 17th-century stairway; and also, partly hidden by the stair, stonework that dates from an earlier gatehouse.*

Prior Rowland Leschman, his cowl over his face, on his tomb in his chantry chapel. Photograph by Stan Beckensall.

The Leschman Chapel. Three of the sculptured figures now below the chapel in the North Aisle, which probably served as corbels in a 13th-century building. They include a vigorous lion, a bagpiper, and a fox preaching to geese, usually supposed to be a mockery of the friars for leading astray the common people. Photograph by Stan Beckensall.

confirmed, but most of the estates had suffered from the war, and a survey of priory lands and properties in the 1370s showed that much was still waste and bringing in only reduced income. Despite all these problems, the canons were able at last to resume work on the church. The wealthy Newcastle merchant Roger Thornton left money to rebuild their nave, and they at least made a start on it. In the middle of the 14th century they added an eastern chapel, beyond the high altar; then they had to ask the Archbishop for land in the Market Place so that they could extend their precinct wall to give room for processing around it. But new building was modest in comparison with the richly carved and painted furnishings added during the 15th century. There were chantry chapels to commemorate Sir Robert Ogle, who died in 1410, and Prior Rowland Leschman, who died in 1491, the latter in particular adorned with stone sculpture and intricately carved wooden tracery as well as having a fine effigy of the Prior himself with his cowl over his face. There were new stalls for the canons with tip-up seats and misericord ledges underneath to ease the long hours of prayer. There were carved wooden canopies above the stalls, and though most went later for firewood surviving fragments may have been incorporated in the font cover. There were paintings, including the array of early Hexham saints looking just like 15th-century bishops. And early in the 16th century a substantial new wooden screen was built to separate the canons from the lay congregation. The screen survives. Though its rood loft early lost its great crucifixion group, and the silver-gilt saints were removed from the line of niches below it, the screen still has most of its painted saints and bishops, its Visitation and Annunciation scenes, and the

The Smythson Screen (sometimes called the Pulpitum or the Rood Screen) as it appears in Hodges' 19th-century drawing, here much reduced. Below the empty niches the row of paterae has the initials O P A D T S P H E Q F H O: 'Pray for the soul of Master Thomas Smythson, Prior of this church, who made this work'. Below are the richly carved doors which could be closed for the canons' private worship, and the painted bishops and saints.

inscription left by its builder, Prior Smythson. Nowadays it supports the Phelps organ installed in 1974.

When the Smythson screen was built, the 16th century and the Tudor dynasty had arrived. The canons at the Priory and the whole north of England faced fresh disruption as Tudor rulers sought to impose a new centralised order. Provincial separatism was to end, and provincial magnates like the Percys and Nevilles had to be brought under Westminster control and learn to respect the King's councillors and ministers. Equally, the autonomy of the Church and its loyalty to Rome was to be destroyed. Both developments would advance the strength of the monarchy and its wealth, for confiscated lands and properties provided vast new royal resources. So the Tudor rulers, and Henry VIII in particular, set about undermining potential opponents, goading them into provincial or ecclesiastical rebellion, then crushing them ruthlessly. The North was effectively rid of the old Scottish menace after Flodden in 1513, but it left the region with a legacy of disorder and violence that was soon redirected against the new threat from overbearing officials, ecclesiastical reformers, and southern progressiveness. Tudor officials and ministers mistrusted northerners at every level, from the great earls in their castles to country folk at market. The Bishop of Carlisle complained to the Archbishop of York that thieves robbed both poor farmers and gentlemen when they came to Hexham market, and their victims 'dare nother complayne of them nor say oone word to them'. Thomas, Lord Dacre, as the Archbishop's Bailiff, strove to rule the unruly tenants of the Regality with a heavy hand, extracting stiff rents, imprisoning troublemakers, and burning the homes of those who fled.

By 1536 King Henry's assault on the Church was under way, and smaller monastic houses were under threat. On 28th September two royal commissioners rode into Hexham to enquire on the state of the Priory; they were deeply interested both in the canons' wealth and in their potentially treasonable attitude towards royal policies, two very good reasons for putting an end to their house. News of the commissioners' coming had spread; the great bells of town and priory were rung, and the townspeople gathered, bearing sticks and halberds, ready to support the canons. When Lionel Gray and Robert Collingwood rode through the crowd to the Priory gate, they found it shut against them; looking down on them from its roof was one of the canons, the master of Ovingham, 'in harness, with a bow bent with arrows'. He refused the king's men entry, saying 'We be 20 brethren in this house, and we shall die ere that ye shall have the house'. Other ostentatiously armed canons appeared, and the hostile crowd must have had Gray and Collingwood looking nervously over their shoulders. They retreated, and the canons hurried them along by following with an armed force some sixty strong.

Within two months the whole of the North was ablaze with rebellion; in the Pilgrimage of Grace loyalty to the old faith was inextricably mixed with provincialism and magnate ambitions. Hexham was fortunate to keep out of the trouble, though two disaffected Percy brothers and the crafty John Heron of Chipchase did their best to bring it in. Hexham and the canons were saved from royal vengeance by the manoevres of a particularly unsavoury royal supporter and sworn foe of Heron, Sir Reynold Carnaby of Halton, Bailiff of Hexham. Thanks to his efforts and the arrival of a royal army under the Duke of Norfolk the Priory was peacefully dissolved in March 1537 and the canons pensioned off. Carnaby's reward was the Priory's local lands and properties, though he did not live long to enjoy them. He and his family moved into the former prior's lodging; he set up his coat of arms on the wall with the date mcccccxxxix (1539) close to the ornate window that Prior Leschman had earlier inserted. Both arms and window remain in the much rebuilt 'Carnaby Building'.

Thirty years later came the last Northern Rebellion against Tudor government when in 1569 the Percy Earl of Northumberland and the Neville Earl of Westmorland were goaded into conspiring against Queen Elizabeth, and rather to their surprise found themselves heading a popular rising. Royal servants in the North led by the redoubtable March Warden Sir John Forster organized loyal forces, and briefly Hexham figured in the dying phases of the rebellion as first Forster, then the Earls, and finally the royal army appeared in the town. The Queen's army stayed in Hexham over Christmas, complaining of bitter frost and snow, before moving on westward to crush the last of the rebels at Naworth.

In 1603 James VI of Scotland became James I of England, and the Border Marches became the Middle Shires. It was a long time before the legacy of violence was finally forgotten, and still longer before the North ceased to be the most impoverished and backward part of the country. But Hexham was at last out of the front line and could develop as a small but peaceful market town.

*Rowland Leschman inserted this window in beautifying the Prior's Lodging about 1480-90, and it was preserved as part of the house that took its place. Above is his monogram, **r l**, in a St Andrew's cross. Photograph by Stan Beckensall.*

The south side of the Market Place in 1634. Peter Ryder's reconstruction shows the ruinous remnant of St Mary's Chapel, with town houses, shops and a bakehouse erected inside and outside its walls. Reproduced by courtesy of Paxton's fish and chip shop, which now occupies the site.

4. PROVINCIAL BACKWATER

Nearly five centuries have passed since Hexham lost its priory, nearly four since it ceased to be frontier town. Though no longer in the forefront of history, it remained the market and administrative hub of a wide area. In most ways its development matched that of any other provincial town; but, as with every such town, Hexham's story also had distinctive features of its own.

For a start, Hexham is in the north of England, and though the 17th-century North was no longer a border country plagued by endemic warfare the legacy of troubled centuries remained. The North was well known to be backward and impoverished, its inhabitants uncouth and prone to violence. Curious visitors from the south like Roger North, Celia Fiennes and Daniel Defoe reported as though on a primitive foreign country; but they also noted that a new kind of life was stirring on Tyneside. Newcastle and the lower river were closely linked to London by busy sea-routes, and Tyneside flourished increasingly from Elizabeth's reign as new coal-burning industries lined the riverside and growing coal shipments went to keep the capital warm and working.

But while the north-east coast grew richer and more civilized, the wild and hilly interior remained primitive, and Hexham was identified with the bare moorlands rather than with urban and industrial development. The town and its residents were regarded with some contempt both by visitors from outside and by the pace-setters in commerce, culture, religion and politics who flourished in booming, progressive Newcastle. Hexham people in their turn, with slow-growing interests in local commerce and manufacture, producing hats, shoes, woollen cloth and above all gloves, wanted to distance themselves from the suspicions still clinging to the wild men of the Border dales; but material growth and cultural development were limited by the inadequacy of their links with the outside. The awfulness of the Northumberland road system and the lack of a good river crossing at Hexham frightened off both visitors and trade. Fortunately, these defects also saved the town from the plundering armies of Scots and English that threatened the region once more during the 17th-century civil wars. Carlisle and Newcastle both suffered lengthy sieges and Scottish occupations; Hexham, though visiting military experts in the 1630s and '40s waxed enthusiastic about the defensive potential of its two towers, remained untouched by war.

However, in the following century Hexham actually played a significant part in the two Jacobite rebellions, partly because local conservatism made it a haven for Catholics and Jacobites, and partly just because the local roads were so awful. In 1715 the Dilston estates of the Catholic Earl of Derwentwater were a base for rebellion, and the Pretender James III was proclaimed in Hexham Market Place. A few local men joined the cause, but the rebels' plans were ill-made and they wandered aimlessly around Northumberland before returning to camp near Hexham and finally going off to defeat at Preston. Derwentwater's execution left lingering local sympathy in the town, as well as unrepentent and disgruntled Jacobites who sometimes came to blows with loyal government supporters when rival taverns turned out. Thirty years later, in November 1745,

James III proclaimed in Hexham Market Place; the engraved vignette is contemporary, but not by an eyewitness.

Marshal Wade, bringing a royal army from Newcastle to intercept the Jacobite attack on Carlisle, took two difficult days to reach Hexham, camped on Kingshaw Green, then found that rain and snow made further progress impossible. The Jacobite army duly took Carlisle, and went forward to brief success. Wade may well have grumbled that Tynedale roads needed radical improvement to match the standard he had set in the Highlands, and not long after his death a new Military Road (now B 6318) was planned to carry army and other traffic speedily from east to west.

One attraction for the Jacobites was the lingering Catholicism of Tynedale, centred in Hexham, which was to sophisticated Novocastrians and suspicious governments proof of the town's backwardness and political unreliability. The old religion had been driven underground almost everywhere, but in Hexham Catholics remained respected leaders of local society. There were Catholic Stewards (or Bailiffs) serving the Fenwick Lords of the Manor, who were themselves staunchly loyal to the house of Stuart until the last Sir John Fenwick was beheaded by William III in 1697 for his flamboyant Jacobitism. The Catholics, led by priests drawn from local landed families, kept an active presence and a mass house in the poor industrial suburb of Cockshaw, part of which consequently became known as Holy Island.

The Catholics were not unchallenged, and amid the religious turmoil in the middle of the 17th century other varieties of faith found a foothold in Hexham; there were Scotch Presbyterians, Quakers and Baptists. The last were involved in a celebrated scandal of 1653, when Thomas Tillam, who had set up a Baptist church in the town, claimed the Rabbi Joseph ben Israel as a notable convert, much to the disgust of the rival Baptist community in Newcastle. In a bitter pamphlet war the rabbi was revealed to a 'False Jew', a Scot named Thomas Ramsay; the upstart Tillam and his rural congregation were duly humiliated. Thereafter, all denominations in the town tacitly accepted the leadership of two remarkable incumbents at the Abbey, the Bohemian-born George Ritschel and his son, also George, who served as curates and lecturers from 1655 to 1717 and were widely respected for their political shrewdness, learning and humanity.

Religion, and the Archbishop of York's concern over the lack of sound Church of England indoctrination, were responsible for giving Hexham a new Grammar School in 1599. Tudor centralisation had placed the Regality in Crown hands in 1545, and finally ended separate jurisdiction in 1572 when Hexhamshire was brought into the County of Northumberland. Lordship of the Manor passed into secular hands, first granted by the Crown and thereafter passing by inheritance or purchase from Sir Christopher Hatton to Sir John Forster and on to his Fenwick

The Grammar School, as it was in the middle of the 19th century, from a Gibson photograph. The headmaster's house is on the right. Courtesy of Tynedale Museums.

descendants and ultimately to the wealthy Blackett family of Newcastle and Wallington. Ecclesiastically Hexhamshire continued in the York diocese, and as the dissolution of the Priory had put an end to whatever education the canons had provided, both Church and townspeople felt the need for a sound Christian school. With a governing body drawn from local landowning gentry and the leaders of trade and industry, the school was to be conducted by a master skilled in Latin and Greek and faithful to the Church of England; in fact, he was usually an ordained minister and sometimes doubled as curate at the Abbey Church. Thereafter at least some of the boys of Hexham and the countryside around were soundly educated on classical and Christian principles, though it was nearly a century before a proper schoolroom was built for them in Hallgate.

St Andrew's was, as visitors often remarked, no more than a decayed and decrepit shadow of its former greatness, lacking a nave and ending abruptly at the crossing; inside, it looked bleak and dull in comparison with its multi-coloured past. It survived as parish church by grace of the Lord of the Manor, who had taken up residence in the former cloistral buildings. Carnaby, Forster, the Fenwicks and the Blacketts successively used the rebuilt Prior's Lodging as a home, proudly renaming it 'Hexham Abbey'. The church alongside, henceforth the Abbey Church, survived in the care of a single curate, who was supported from 1628 by a lecturer paid from funds provided by the London Company of Mercers. Sometimes one man held both offices, and generally Curate and Lecturer worked together until the two posts were permanently combined in the 19th century, and the incumbent finally became a Rector.

The town around the Abbey Church showed few signs of growth. Most houses were now of stone with thatched roofs; Celia Fiennes, riding round England on her side-saddle in 1698, was the most complimentary of its visitors, describing Hexham as 'one of the best towns in Northumberland ... its built of

Holy Island House, *with the date 1657 over its doorway. This was the largest house in the industrial suburb, and served as a Catholic mass house. Photograph by Brian Jenkins.*

The George and Dragon, St Mary's Chare. The Inn was one of half a dozen in Back Street, whose gentle curve shows its origin, outside the Priory wall; the 17th-century deeds all refer to stone-built houses with thatched roofs, each backing on to the 'the Abbey Orchard Wall'. Photograph by Brian Jenkins.

stone and looks very well ... many streetes, some are pretty broad all well pitch'd with a spacious Market place with a Town Hall on the Market Cross'. Building fashions remained perhaps half a century behind those in more progressive parts, with older materials in use long after brick, tile and slate had succeeded them elsewhere. Holy Island

House, with its lintel dated 1657, retained mullioned windows in Tudor style; and other surviving 17th-century frontages in Market Street look distinctly Elizabethan. But the George and Dragon, one of many inns serving those who came to market, and the Grammar School, both from the last two decades of the century, were more sophisticated.

The pattern of local administration was another of Hexham's peculiarities; though here again most country towns had their own traditional way of doing things. Officially, Hexham was never a borough; with no charter from king or archbishop, it was simply a conglomeration of hamlets within the Regality which had now become wards: Market Steads, Priestpopple, Hencotes, and Gilligate, including Cockshaw. That did not stop the inhabitants thinking and writing of Hexham as a borough. The Guild of Skinners and Glovers, drawing up new rules in 1613, affirmed proudly that they dwelt in an 'antient borrough', the Borough Court dealt with town issues, and the Borough Book kept a record of its decisions. Ultimate responsibility for local affairs stayed with the Lord of the Manor as successor to the Archbishop; but the King's judges now dealt with criminal cases from Hexham, on occasion at Hexham but more usually at Newcastle and Morpeth; and the County JPs gradually infiltrated the affairs of the Shire until by the 18th century they regularly met in quarter sessions or petty sessions at the Moot Hall. Most local problems were settled by the Manor Court or the Borough Court, presided over by the Lord of the Manor or his Steward, and each made up of the local gentry or leading citizens who would elsewhere have become JPs.

The cases before the Borough Court give the fullest picture of the townsfolk and their preoccupations during these centuries, though the Court overlapped in both personnel and function with such bodies as the four trade guilds (Skinners and Glovers, Tanners and Shoemakers, Weavers, Hatters) and the 'Four and Twenty' (or parish vestry), chosen six from each ward. The Court dealt with all sorts of petty nuisances and misbehaviour: scolding, eavesdropping, immorality, polluting streams or pant, leaving rubbish about, allowing beasts to stray, causing fire hazards. It was also much concerned over incomers or foreigners, particularly if they were so impoverished that they or their bastard children might become a charge on the parish; and particularly if they were Scots, who were said to have become 'very insolent, proud, haughtty, and sawcey in their carryage, behavor and language'. Such vagrants might be expelled unless a householder took responsibility for them, though occasionally there was a more charitable alternative; in 1655 a vagrant named Macconell was given a job as swineherd, while others were regularly employed as a team of scalerakers, or scavengers, to keep the town and the Market Place clean. The Court paid these, and other public servants such as the common keepers who supervised livestock on the open fields, from market dues. Most public servants, however, were unpaid, part-time, and sometimes unreliable: the constables for each ward, the market keepers and ale tasters, the pant keeper in charge of the water supply, and the highway surveyors.

Overlooking the Market Place were tall houses, replacing the former Priory wall on one side, lining the frontage of the Town Hall (or Sessions House, the present Moot Hall) on the other. Some were the town houses of local gentry, and on the south side was the residence of the Allgood family from Nunwick, whose influence in the town matched that of the Blackett Lords of the Manor. It was Robert Allgood who in 1703 provided a new pant, or public water supply, the focal point for the market over the next century and a half; and Sir Lancelot Allgood who as High Sheriff and MP represented authority and loyalty during the difficult years of Jacobitism and the Hexham Riot.

Sir Lancelot Allgood, a respected establishment figure, nevertheless met much local hostility. He had a particularly bitter critic in Anne Cook, landlady of the 'Black Bull' and proprietress of the town's assembly rooms, on the opposite side of the Market Place at the head of Bull (or Hallstile) Bank. Its hosts were notoriously Catholic, and Sir Lancelot suspected the inn was a hotbed of Jacobitism. There were frequent disputes, as when the Cooks led the objections to Sir Lancelot's intention to close down Hexham Races, where he feared Jacobite conspirators might gather. In 1745 Anne and her husband were finally forced to leave for Morpeth, so that their daughter was left to entertain the officers of Marshal Wade's army when they were billeted in the town. Anne Cook sought an unusual revenge by launching a cookery book. It was packed with large and tasty dishes to whet substantial 18th-century appetites, but good recipes were submerged by her overflowing bitterness. Her main purpose was to pour scorn on the best-selling cookery book published by Hannah Glasse, who happened to be Sir Lancelot's half-sister, and much of Anne's book was a plaintive and bitter attack on those who had so sorely persecuted unfortunate Catholic innkeepers.

The tensions and mutual mistrust were partly religious, partly social and political. Within the town, most people readily accepted the authority of the landed gentry, and welcomed the benevolent paternalism of the Lord of the Manor Sir Walter Blackett, who graciously opened his landscaped grounds on the Seal in 1753, and provided market traders with a covered 'piazza' (later the 'Shambles') in 1766. But outside there was more cause for concern. The growth of lead-mining and smelting in the countryside to north and south, and particularly on Sir Walter's Allendale estates, brought growing numbers of rural industrial workers into the vicinity of Hexham to add an element of class conflict. Sir Lancelot, Sir Walter and their friends of the law-abiding establishment had doubts about such workers. In 1761 this mistrust contributed to an explosion of violence that became the Hexham Riot, alternatively known as the Hexham Insurrection or the Hexham Massacre.

England was at war with France, and the government had, in 1757, regularised the recruitment of a county militia by arranging a triennial ballot for selection from the names of eligible young men listed by the constables. The force selected would train for twenty days a year over its three-year term, and stand ready to deal with home defence or public order. The thought of such compulsory service naturally roused hostility, particularly among craftsmen and industrial workers, who had generally avoided it under the more haphazard system of nomination by local landowners. When the second round of balloting got under way early in 1761 organized opposition developed in the North, and, by dint of public demonstration wherever the county magistrates met to conduct the ballot, successfully defied the law. At Gateshead in February the magistrates abandoned the ballot; at Morpeth early in March they faced violence from a mob, and at least one gentleman suffered a broken head before they gave in. There was similar surrender to force at Belford, Whittingham and Etal.

Then the authorities decided that they must take a stand, at the well publicised meeting due on 9th March at Hexham. The problem was that common folk had no way of expressing discontent other than by public demonstration, all too likely to turn to riot; while the authorities had no machinery for keeping order apart from the very militia for which they sought recruits. In readiness for the expected trouble, they brought six companies of the North Yorkshire Militia to Hexham, and posted them in the Market Place in front of the Sessions House where they met. Throughout the morning the Militia stood fast, while detachments of workers from all all over Tynedale marched into the crowded Market Place with banners flying and horns blowing. Fearful militia officers numbered the crowd at an impossible five thousand, though more sober reports placed them at several hundreds. The magistrates eventually brought matters to a head by reading the Riot Act, bidding the crowd disperse or face the use of force; the militia now knew they had authority to open fire, the leaders of the crowd that they must act now or never. Shots were fired, perhaps first from the crowd for an officer and a militiaman were killed; and then the militia drew back, presented, fired, and continued firing. The Market Place was littered with bloody corpses, and the ultimate total death roll was 51; it included only eight from Hexham itself, of whom two were women. Shocked but self-righteous, the county establishment expressed its views through the pulpit; throughout Northumberland the clergy preached and published ringing condemnations of the irresponsible, unchristian and traitorous behaviour of the mob. The popular movement was crushed, and one of the Morpeth ringleaders was duly hanged though none of the Hexham survivors suffered more than a brief imprisonment or a shilling fine.

Perhaps the most remarkable feature of this dramatic tragedy was the speed with which it was forgotten, at a time when the media presented only establishment views. It was the most violent event on English soil between the skirmishes of the '45 Rebellion and the 1780 Gordon Riots, when some 800 people died because magistrates and militia hesitated too long before taking action. Yet the Hexham Riot has left little trace in the history books, and, even more surprisingly, no public monument or record in the town.

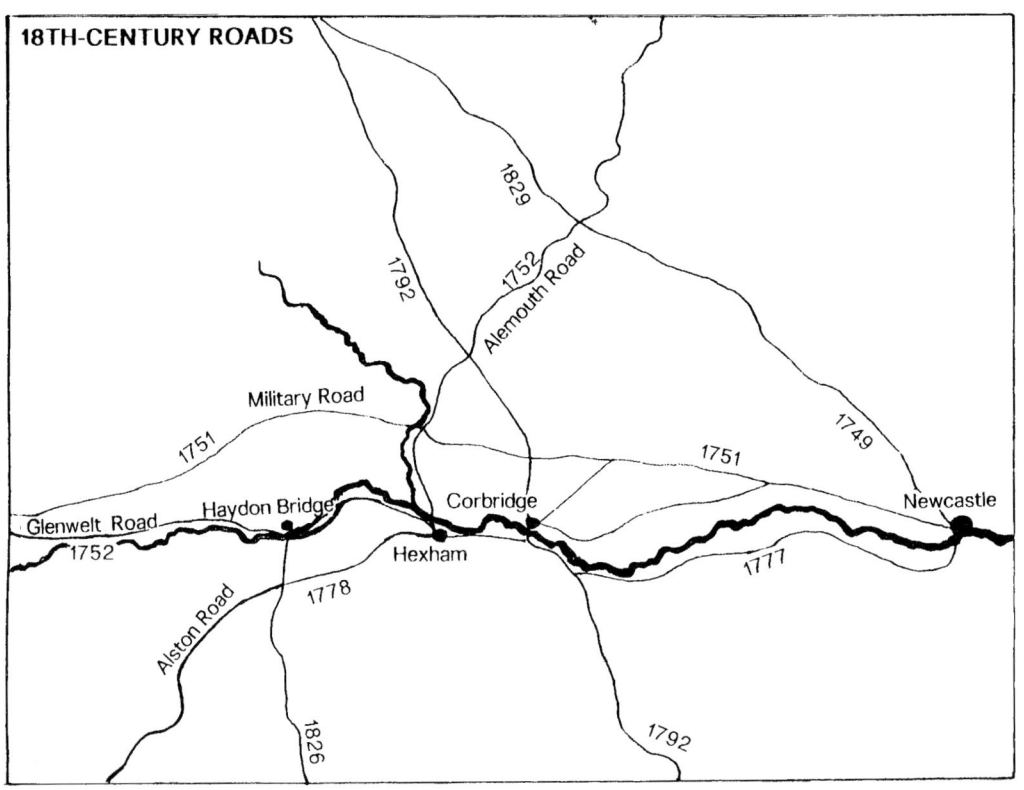

New roads of the 18th century. The date of the first act authorising each road is given.

5. Renewal

Over the later decades of the 18th century and the first of the 19th revolutionary changes in transport put an end to the isolation of Hexham, and brought it closer to the economic and social dynamo of the lower Tyne. These changes followed growing demand from the cities, ports and industries of coast and riverside for the minerals and farm produce of Tynedale. There, lead-working, coal, leather, corn, vegetable and fruit growing were all expanding, as were the markets for these products on Tyneside and beyond. New links were needed, so turnpike roads criss-crossed the county from the 1750s, and Hexham revived as a meeting-point, market and overnight stop for the waggons and coaches that used them. Lead and corn production was growing on the wide estates of such landowners as Sir Walter Blackett, and it was these gentlemen who led

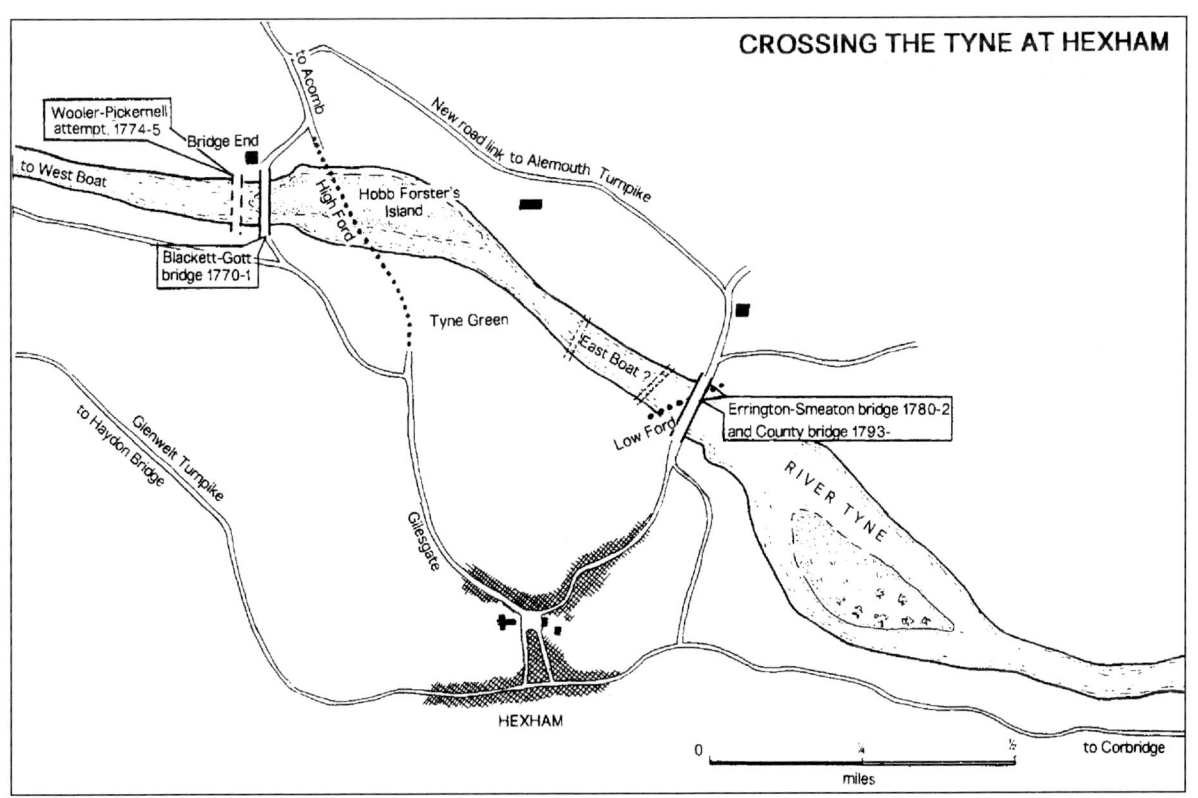

Crossing the Tyne. *The complex story of the 18th-century attempts to bridge the Tyne at Hexham.*

The bridge in ruins. This engraving of 1782 shows the disastrous collapse of the Smeaton-Errington bridge after the blizzard of March 1782. The masonry and the design were used, on much more substantial foundations, when the bridge was rebuilt and opened in 1793.

the campaign to build good roads to the lower Tyne and the coastal ports. The cross-country 'Military Road' (B6318) was planned in 1751 and completed in 1757; it cost £24,000 and was built in part from the stones of Hadrian's Wall. The 'Alemouth' or 'Corn Road' (A6079-B6342/6341) passed through Sir Walter's great estates on its way to the grain-shipping port of Alnmouth. The 'Glenwelt Turnpike' linked Hexham to the west on a route later followed in part by the A69. The last major road improvement planned at Hexham during the turnpike era was an improved western link, though its intended route from the town centre across the Seal was rejected in 1823 when a popular petition against it won over the Lady of the Manor, Mrs Beaumont; the cherished open space so graciously opened to townsfolk half a century before by her predecessor Sir Walter Blackett was preserved intact, and instead the road crossed the Cockshaw Burn by a new bridge to Shafto Leazes and Quatre Bras.

The Alemouth Road set off on its north-easterly way not from Hexham but from the turnpike bar at Acomb; to reach the road travellers from Hexham had to wade across the High Ford. The road-makers intended to link up with Hexham by building a bridge to supersede the two Tyne fords and the two boats, which had long carried travellers but were slow and dangerous when the river was high. The tragi-comic tale of Hexham's bridge

The Tyne Bridge. Smeaton's bridge as rebuilt on a fully paved river bed in 1793. Since reinforced and widened, the bridge has carried fast-growing heavy traffic for two centuries. In 1993 a plaque honouring the engineers involved was unveiled, naming John Smeaton and Robert Mylne as designers, with Robert Thompson and William Johnson, Bridge Surveyors for the county. Photograph by Ben Bolt.

The bandstand in the Abbey Grounds, presented to the town in 1912 by Henry Bell. Photograph by Tynedale Planning Department.

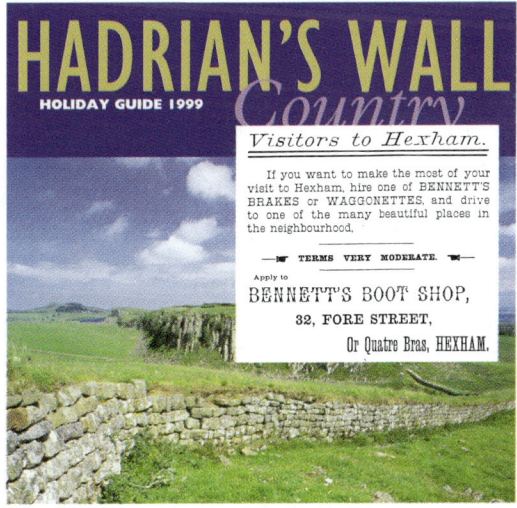

Tourist Literature, ancient and modern.

The changing Hexham home.

These houses show dwellings built in Hexham since 1825, for changing social groups and needs: 1. About 1825, Orchard Place. 2. About 1900, Shaftoe Crescent (Photograph, Rodney Higginns). 3. About 1936, Hextol Crescent. 4. About 1948, Priestlands Avenue. 5. About 1983, Eastwood Grange estate. 6. 1988, Abbey Court, retirement apartments.

began when the rising Yorkshire engineer John Smeaton drew an elegant design in 1756, but fund-raising proved difficult and it was left to Sir Walter Blackett to find both the money and another Yorkshire bridge-builder, William Gott, who started work in 1767. Gott's effort was competent, but it coincided fatally with Tynedale's greatest natural disaster, when the river bed proved unstable and the river prone to violent flooding. It crossed where the river narrowed just above the High Ford, and travellers approached it, as they had the ford, by way of Gilesgate, now Tyne Green Road. Opened with joyful pomp by Sir Walter in 1770, it was swept away in the calamitous flood of November 1771. On that occasion Hexham was by no means the only casualty, for the flood destroyed every bridge over the Tyne save that at Corbridge. It also ruined the market gardeners, millers and wheelwrights on Tyne Green below the bridge, and drowned 230 sheep on Anick Haugh across the river.

Work started on a second bridge almost at once fifty yards upstream, but the ground proved treacherous and swallowed the piers as fast as they were erected, so the attempt was abandoned. Next, Smeaton (by now the most celebrated engineer of the day) tried again. He had misgivings from the start, but looked for better luck at a site down river near the Low Ford. He proposed to use construction methods very different from Gott's, assuming rather unfairly that Gott's errors had contributed more than the forces of nature to the disaster. Smeaton's bridge was completed early in 1781. A little over a year later, in March 1782, it broke up in a blizzard as torrents scoured deep between the piers and pushed over Smeaton's stonework. It was the one failure of a famous career, and it threatened ruin for Henry Errington of Sandhoe who had financed it. Public enquiries and disputes followed before the county authorities set about replacing Smeaton's bridge on the site he had chosen, having first laid paving across the entire river bed and secured it with deep piles. Robert Thompson and William Johnson, the county bridge surveyors, spared no expense to re-erect the bridge on these firm foundations, and had it working by 1793 though it was two more years before it was fully opened to traffic. With subsequent strengthening and widening, Smeaton's stately bridge on its reinforced base still stands.

Since the bulk of Tynedale's trade passed along the valley rather than across it, the bridge made relatively little difference. By that time transport fashions were changing and plans were afoot to move Tynedale produce by canal. In the 1790s three rival canal routes were proposed and surveyed, but this left high-level enthusiasts arguing with low, and south-bankers opposing north-siders. They criticised one another so forcefully that confidence in all the schemes evaporated, and nobody subscribed. The fiasco did not stop ambitious trans-Pennine canal proposals surfacing again from time to time over the next two centuries.

Canal-worship gave way to railway mania, and the Tyne Valley was early recognized as ideal for a cross-country route. The Newcastle and Carlisle Railroad Company was formed in 1825 and began construction in 1829. By the end of 1834 waggon-trains were carrying lead along it from Hexham to the refineries at Blaydon, and by 1835 passengers were not only travelling to and from Tyneside but were being pulled by steam locomotives, which had been originally excluded from the line. By 1838 the railway was working along its full length, and steam trains crossing the country from sea to sea called at Hexham station. The dashing stage-coaches which had for a few decades made good use of the turnpikes and paused on their way at Hexham's colourful menagerie of White Hart and White Horse, Black Bull and Grey Bull, were instantly superseded. The former road centre became a railway junction as lines were built to tap the coal of the North Tyne and the lead of Allendale in the 1860s. Tynedale's lead and corn, Hexham's leather, apples, and fresh vegetables now found their way by rail to supply the demand from expanding towns down river. Before long there came traffic in reverse, as those who worked on Tyneside chose to live in Tynedale, and these incomers often built themselves large houses on the fringes of the town, soberly classical at Halliwell Dene, Orchard House, Temperley House or the Leazes; or exuberantly Gothic at Duke's House, a country home built in the woods for the Sunderland banker Edward Backhouse.

Once better links had been established with the outside world, Hexham population grew more steadily, no longer so subject to the vagaries of food shortage and the nastier epidemics. Numbers in the town rose from 3,427 in 1801 to 7,071 at the end of the century; but this was modest in comparison with the phenomenal growth rates in the country as a whole and industrial towns in particular. Whereas just over one per cent of the North-East's population lived in Hexham at the start of the century, less than half of one

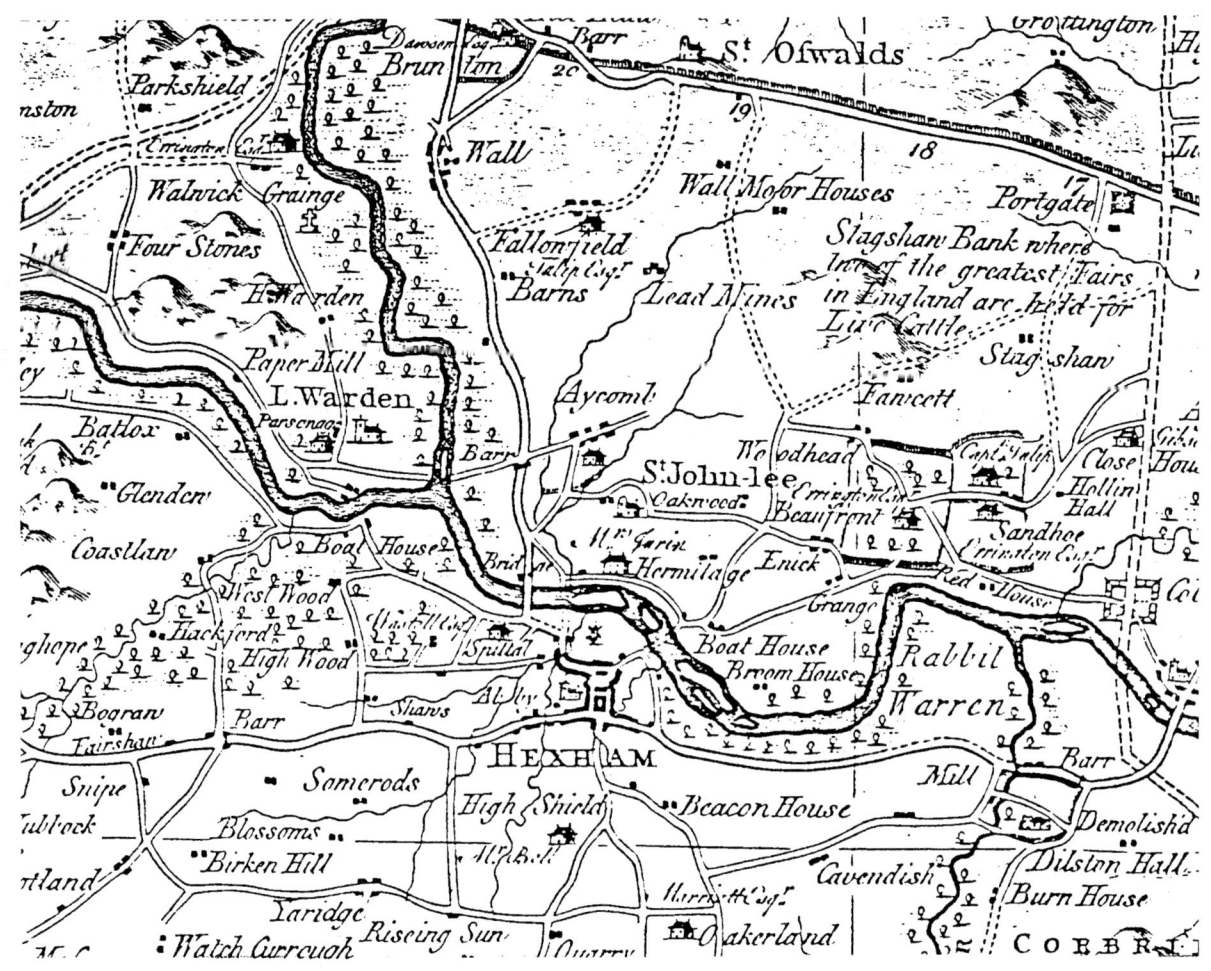

Armstrong's map of Northumberland, published in 1769, shows the short-lived bridge, and the turnpike 'barrs' around the town.

The Market Place about 1864, after the 'White Horse' had been demolished and replaced by shops (now the Edinburgh Woollen Mill) and while the public pant still occupied its central place in the life of the town. Photograph by courtesy of Tynedale Museums.

per cent were there at its end. Like so many other small towns that had once been centres of economic and cultural progress throughout the land, Hexham was something of an anachronism in industrial Britain.

At first the slowly rising population simply crowded more densely into the old town centre. Every old street had its subsidiary nicks and alleys and courts, while almost every old house was subdivided into one-

Hexham Station, as shown in Carmichael's print of the early days on the Newcastle to Carlisle Railway.

room tenements. Shops lined the narrow streets; the directories list bakers, bookbinders, brass founders, butchers, cabinet makers, cartwrights, china dealers, cloggers, confectioners, coopers, curriers, druggists, dyers, engravers, fellmongers, glovers, grocers, hatters, innkeepers, ironmongers, joiners, linen drapers, maltsters, milliners, printers, ropemakers, sundry dealers, tailors, tallow chandlers, tanners, tawyers, watchmakers, weavers, wine merchants, with scores of other tradesmen and craftsmen who worked in the back room behind the shop and lived cosily with their families above it, keeping a lodger or two in the spare room and housing the servants in the attics. The teeming life of Hexham town centre was celebrated in the autobiography of Joseph Parker, who was born in St Mary's Chare in 1830 and earned national fame as a Congregationalist minister and an outstanding preacher at the City Temple. He remembered with affection 'quaint old Hexham ... its old-world market-place, its ever-flowing pant ... its narrow streets, its environs of green undulations ... thriving tradesmen, the Mechanics' Institute where I borrowed my first books ...'

Hexham residents might relish their sheltered life but others viewed the town more critically. To outsiders Hexham often appeared mean, backward, dirty and lacking in common amenities, its dwellings small, low and ill ventilated, its people ignorant, idle and dissipated. Part of the problem lay in the lack

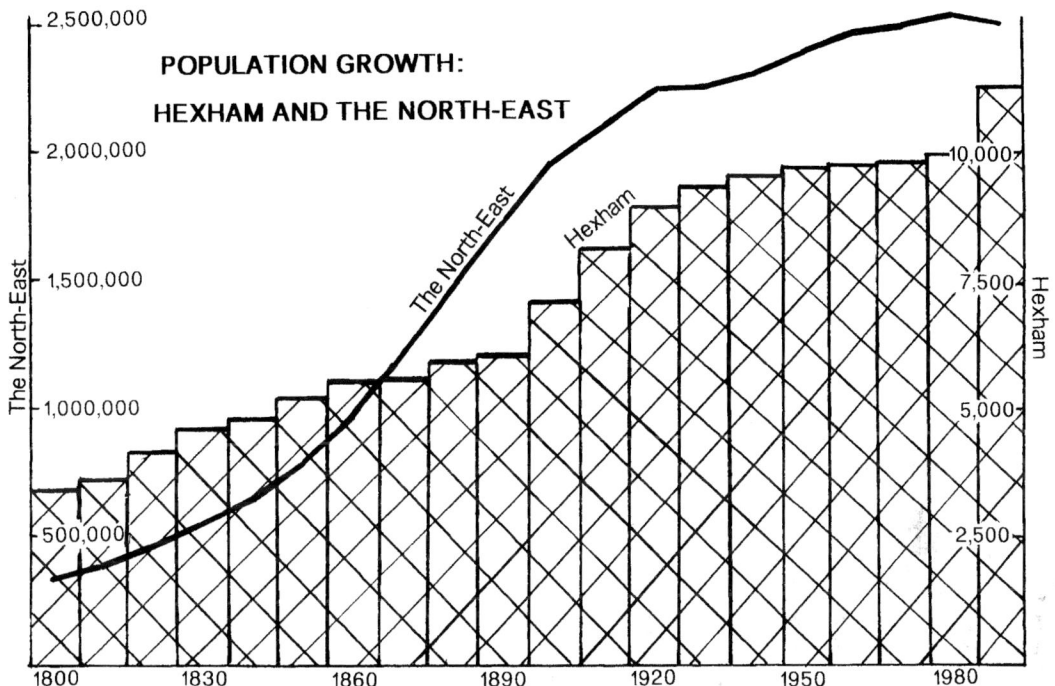

The steady growth of numbers living in Hexham contrasts with the rapid rise of population in the North-East region as a whole. In 1800 just over 1% of the North-East's 320,000 people lived in Hexham; now it is less than 0.5% of two and a half millions. Early in the 19th century, the North-East population grew at 17% each decade, rising to 21% in the second half of the century, while Hexham's decennial growth rate fell from 8% to 6% at the same period. Both local and regional growth rates have slowed almost to a stop in recent decades.

of any modern administrative organization. The Beaumonts as Lords of the Manor took a broadly paternal interest, but they were rarely present in person, preferring their country residence at Bywell and letting their Abbey home to tenants. Their Stewards, supported by out of date institutions like the Borough and Manor Courts, were ill equipped to face the demands of a growing town and increasing pressure from reform-minded governments and public opinion that was fast becoming articulate. Self-help, when public-spirited townsfolk responded to Beaumont encouragement, did something to improve the situation: a Subscription School was started in 1813 for children who found no place in the Grammar School, a Dispensary was set up in 1816 to treat the poor, a Mechanics' Institute and library was busy on Hallstile Bank from 1825. The town was lit by oil lamps in 1824, which were replaced in 1835 when a new gasworks opened in Burn Lane. The community found alternative leadership from the pulpit in a period of religious vigour when denominations multiplied and expanded to meet new needs. Presbyterians, Congregationalists and Wesleyans built themselves new chapels in Hexham, while the socially aware Primitive Methodists (the Ranters) arrived from the lead dales and built a succession of chapels: Hallstile Bank was followed by St Mary's Chare and finally by the Central Chapel on the corner of Beaumont Street. The Roman Catholics, no longer

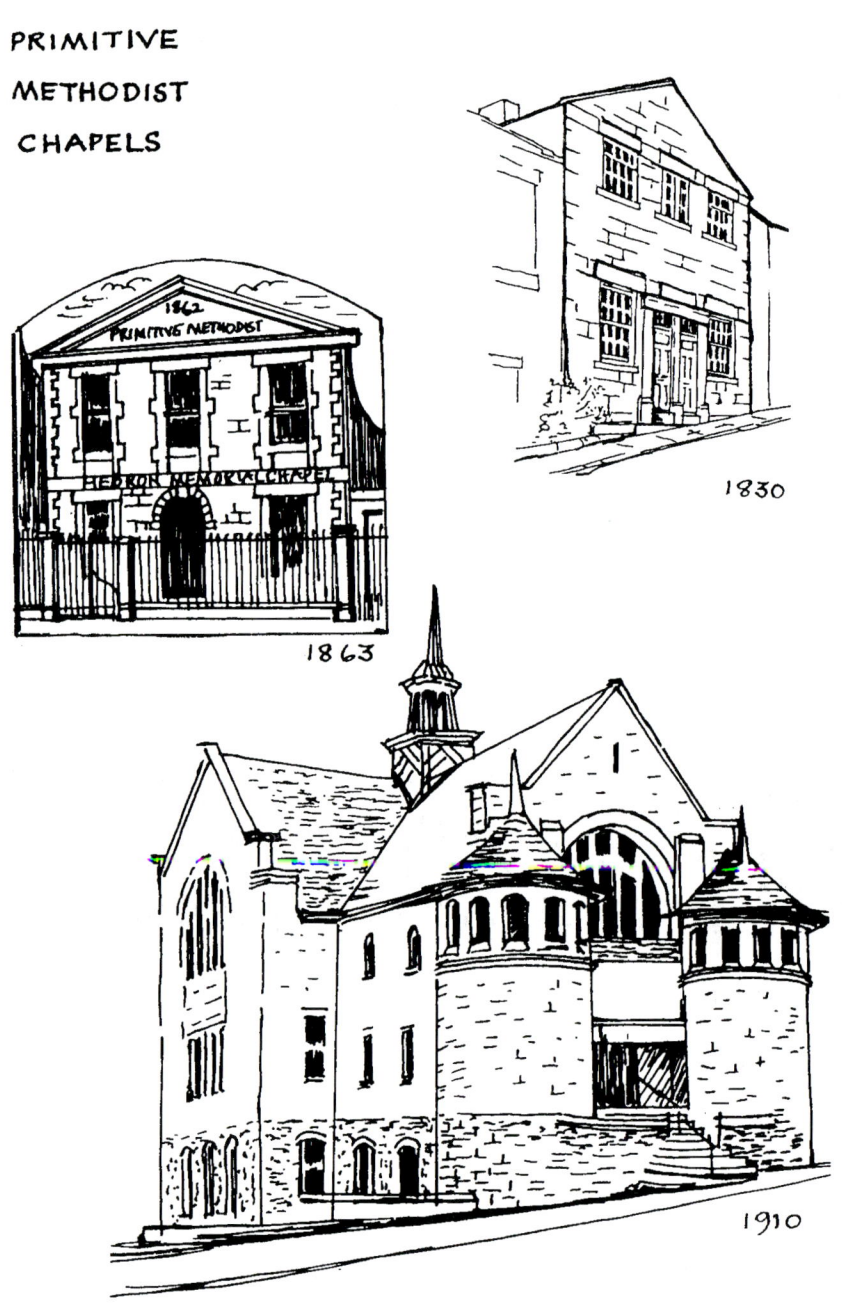

PRIMITIVE METHODIST CHAPELS

1830

1863

1910

The Primitive Methodists *built their first chapel in 1830 on Hallstile Bank, then usually called Bull Bank, from the Black Bull Inn at the top. Thirty years later Elizabeth Hebbron, wealthy widow of a PM preacher, built the elegant Hebbron memorial chapel in Back Street. In 1909 the much larger and very impressive Central Church was built for the Primitives on the prestigious corner of Beaumont Street and Battle Hill. Twenty years later the Methodist groups were united, and in another twenty years they had abandoned their former church. Drawings by Sheila Corfe.*

hiding in the industrial slums, celebrated emancipation by building in 1830 a splendid new St Mary's overlooking Hencotes.

Self-help could not disguise the need for a more up-to-date administration. Reforming governments exerted pressure, first by imposing a national pattern of poor relief. A newly elected Board of Guardians took responsibility for the Hexham Union and built in 1839 a gloomy union workhouse at Peth Head that was submerged a century later in the General Hospital. A Public Health Act followed in 1848, and in its wake came a government inspector to assess the needs and failings of Hexham. His forceful Report, with its pungent criticism of streets, drains, water supply, overcrowding, health care, and general public irresponsibility, finally brought home to Hexham people the inadequacy of existing institutions. Plans were immediately made for an elected Local Board of Health, which from 1854 set about mending the sad state of the town. Within little more than a decade a water supply was piped into every house, first from the Wydon Burn Reservoir constructed during the '60s, later from the Ladle Wells far out in the Shire; the familiar public pant in the Market Place was removed in 1865. Sewerage followed, with a complete system of drains being laid between 1875 and 1878. All these developments were hotly debated in Board elections, and a popular press emerged to meet the popular interest; Beaumont influence and money helped set the *Hexham Courant* going in 1864, and it was soon joined by a Conservative rival, the *Herald*.

*The elegant Gothic interior designed by Father Singleton for the new **Catholic church of St Mary** in 1830.*

The Abbey Grounds are cleared and levelled in preparation for laying out Beaumont Street. In front of the church remains of the crowded buildings recently removed are still visible, and perhaps include the last fragments of the Priory's infirmary. Photograph by courtesy of Tynedale Museums.

The Local Board, with the help of W B Beaumont MP, lord of the Manor, also transformed the town centre. The crowded Market Place, and particularly the buildings crammed around the south-east corner of the Abbey and known as the Long Back Side, had been a particular disgrace in the eyes of hygienically-minded visitors. Some of the higgledy-piggledy houses and workshops had been removed in the 1840s to make way for a rebuilt east end of the Abbey, eventually completed in 1860 by John Dobson; then Beaumont cleared away the rest of the slummy Long Back Side. Finally, in 1864 Beaumont and the Board co-operated in laying out a new street across the Abbey Grounds, a tree-lined boulevard in sharp contrast to the narrow, winding older streets. The Market Place was dramatically opened up, with a broad link stretching to the top of Battle Hill. Beside the new road and on land now cut off from the rest of Beaumont's back garden, the Town Hall and Corn Exchange was built in 1866 in a style reminiscent of contemporary French public buildings. It was the first of a sequence of stolid Victorian buildings (offices, shops, chapels and hotel) looking out over what was left of the Abbey Grounds towards the Seal. The tree-dotted Grounds themselves remained behind a new stone wall, but they were no longer hidden away at the back of crowded housing and had become an integral and attractive part of the townscape. Forty-eight years after Beaumont Street was built, the Abbey Grounds were finally sold to the town to become a public park, an extension to the long-open landscape of the Seal. Beaumont Street has matured over the past century. With the imposing mass of the Abbey Church to close its northern vista, a stately line of buildings facing spacious parkland, and the vigorous statue of the Boer War hero Colonel Benson to oversee its southern end, it constitutes a contribution to the townscape of which the Local Board might justifiably feel proud.

The Local Board did not last long, for local government continued to evolve. In 1874 an elected School Board proceeded to reorganize local education, but it was a process that has hardly ceased since as fresh ideas and initiatives have tumbled over one another. A new Grammar School to replace the ancient building in Hallgate was eventually opened at Fellside in 1910, supplemented by the Sele School (successor since 1856 to the Subscription School). Reorganization in the 1960s moved the Queen Elizabeth High School to a new site at Whetstone Bridge and placed the Middle School at Fellside. New elementary schools provided for younger children, which became successively junior, primary or first schools; while the Catholics, who had opened their original school soon after St Mary's was built, evolved their own pattern of education. Throughout the 19th century and well into the 20th the town's public schools were supplemented by an array of small private establishments run by young men with enthusiasm and a little learning, or by dedicated and impecunious ladies. Complex and confusing the story of Hexham's schools over the past century may be, but they have never failed to provide a sound educational grounding and a literate population.

New national patterns of local government replaced both boards during the 1890s and 1900s. Northumberland County Council took charge of local education, while Urban and Rural District Councils took overall charge of town and Shire from 1894. Under this reorganized management Hexham faced a new century.

The Temperley Memorial Fountain of 1901, with W W Gibson's poem on its north side:

> O you who drink my cooling waters clear
> Forget not the far hills from whence they flow;
> Where over fell and moorland year by year,
> Spring, Summer, Autumn, Winter, come and go,
> With showering sun, and rain, and storm, and snow
> Where over the green bents for ever blow
> The four free winds of Heaven; where time falls
> In solitary places calm and slow.
> Where pipes the curlew and the plover calls,
> Beneath the open sky my waters spring
> Beneath the clear sky welling fair and sweet,
> A draught of coolness for your thirst to bring,
> A sound of coolness in the busy street.

6. TWENTIETH-CENTURY CHALLENGE

Visitors arriving at Hexham by train in the early years of the 20th century were greeted by the scent of apples. Opposite the station they saw the office of Fell & Co, whose nurseries were 'among the largest and best stocked in the North of England'. On the skyline were medieval towers and turrets, and beyond them they could find cobbled streets lined with cosy shops and busy craftsmen, crowded with country folk, animals, a good deal of dirt and some pungent smells. Hexham was still the country town that J P Gibson had depicted in vivid photographs, tightly surrounded by rolling green fields and fairy-tale woods. It had readjusted itself to meet Victorian standards, but it now faced the greater changes and challenges of the 20th century. A new Market Place pant was erected in 'the last year of Queen Victoria and the first of King Edward Vll', but the 20th-century Temperley Memorial Fountain offered free refreshment in contrast to the multi-purpose and essential water supplied by its predecessor. On one side of its decorative pillar the affectionate lines of a young local poet, Wilfrid Wilson Gibson, evoked the windswept moorland from which came the town's improved water supply.

Country towns like Hexham were fortunate to be sheltered from the nastiest aspects of the 20th century, and though the town and its people were deeply affected by two world wars they never experienced bombs or shells. Refugees or evacuees brought a taste of occupied Belgium or blitzed Tyneside, soldiers or prisoners-of-war were familiar sights, money was constantly wanted for troop comforts or war weapons, and all too often the dreaded telegrams brought bitter news. Half the town's menfolk served in the First World War, and one in eight of Hexham's adult males died in it.

The impact of war was fierce but brief. The effects of economic and social change were more far-reaching and longer lasting. The all-embracing greenery of orchard, shrubbery and market garden disappeared as Hexham ceased to feed Tyneside with fruit and vegetables. Some open space by the river was preserved as a golf course, public playground and country park, and the town centre parks blossomed and flourished; but much of the encircling open space vanished under the brick and tarmac of light industry, supermarket and car-park. The fields and wooded slopes behind the town were lost to spacious new housing estates, for the most spectacular change of the last century has been the vast expansion of the built area. Hexham's population continued to grow only slowly, creeping up to 9,700 in the first half of the century and on to over 11,000 in the second; but changing life-styles meant that new housing estates spread at an ever faster pace. First, they surged over Windmill Hill to Quatre Bras, Burswell and Leazes Lane, southward up Elvaston and eastward to Peth Head and White Cross. In the forty years after 1945, as compact terraces gave way to semis and detached housing, the town tripled in size. This undisciplined growth brought concern over the destruction of the countryside, and demands for a green belt to be established around the town.

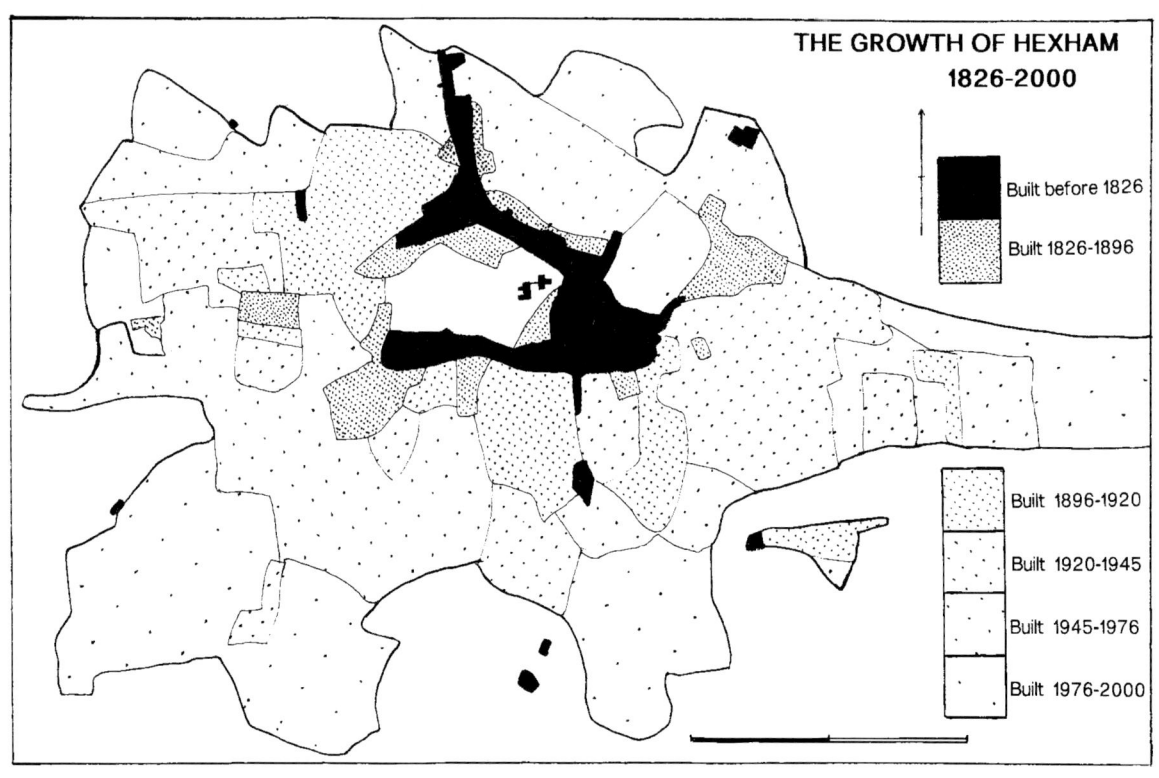

The spread of Hexham in the 19th and 20th centuries.

To cope with urban growth and economic changes there was another renewal of local administration, and in 1974 the former Urban and Rural District Councils were replaced by the Tynedale District Council. Hexham became the administrative centre for an unwieldly area of some 850 square miles that brought together the Border Dales, the Wall country, the South Tyne and the urban ribbon along the river to Prudhoe; and as an administrative centre it attracted other headquarters, such as those of the Northumberland National Park and the English Heritage Hadrian's Wall management team, both well outside their own territory. For the town itself there was at last a mayor and borough council, though their powers and resources were limited.

These new authorities faced social and economic challenges. Many of the older industries like glove-making, tanning, market gardening and the lead-working of the dales faded away in the later years of the 19th century, and new industries took their place in the 20th. The most obtrusive was a large chipboard factory from the 1960s that sprawled and spewed pollutants on the north side of the river, where it was at the heart of a new industrial estate. At about the same time an assortment of smaller businesses, workshops and retail outlets extended over much of the ground once occupied by nurseries, orchards and allotments.

Fortunately the most vigorous growth industry was a more attractive one, as tourism became a major preoccupation for the community as a whole and for local government in particular. Hexham had always attracted visitors setting off to explore the Roman Wall country. The first move to bring them to the town for its own sake came in 1878, when the Tynedale Hydropathic Mansion opened on the hillside above Whetstone Bridge, offering 80 bedrooms, resident physicians, therapeutic water, winter gardens, croquet and lawn tennis; the Hydro had a checkered and usually unsuccessful career before its buildings were eventually absorbed into the Queen Elizabeth High School. Most visitors to Hexham still found its surrounding country more rewarding than the town itself, which was described by a guidebook in 1921 as 'the gate by road and rail to the romantic holiday areas of the N. and S. Tyne valleys, and of Allendale'. Bicycle, car and char-a-banc bore visitors from the town rather than to it, despite public and private efforts to reverse their route. One of the town's prominent monuments, usually known as the Manor Office, was renamed the Old Gaol and developed in the 1970s and '80s as a tourist information office and a museum celebrating the reiving past of the northern dales, but efforts to present the historic attractions of the town as a whole to visitors met with little success. Those who did come tended to show more interest in large-scale shopping centres than in historic buildings and museums. The efforts of the planning, conservation and tourism officers of the District Council, together with the work of an active Civic Society, successfully preserved the more attractive features of the town centre, and stocked with trees, flowers and vistas the parks that chance had left so close to it.

THE TYNEDALE HYDROPATHIC ESTABLISHMENT, HEXHAM.

F. G. GRANT, Proprietor.   Prospectuses on Application.   See Page 100 of this Guide.

The Hydro, as it appeared in the 'Historical Guide' of 1889, which assured readers that 'The sanitary arrangements have recently been much improved, and are now in a thoroughly sound state.'

Hexham's regional role was underlined by new hospital provision in and around the town. From 1902 there was an Infectious Diseases Hospital (the 'Fever Hospital') just south-east of the town, with a smallpox hospital further out at Dipton Wood. The War Memorial Hospital opened in 1921, fully equipped with male, female and children's wards, operating theatre and X-ray room; it survived until 1995. Soon after the start of the 1939 war an Emergency Services Hospital opened on the Corbridge Road, which became the General Hospital after 1945, with a specialist Regional Spinal Unit. As the century neared its end there were plans to rebuild it on the same site, but without its specialism.

The Swimming Baths in Gilesgate, built in 1885 for Henry Bell and Sons, Tanners, Skinners, Wool Staplers and Artificial Manure Manufacturers, as their fleece warehouse, and still showing the date and the Bell Monogram. Photograph by Brian Jenkins.

Some of the 20th-century developments can be epitomised in three buildings associated with the prosperous fellmongering and tanning business headed in its Victorian heyday by Henry Bell. The firm had built in 1885 an imposing wool warehouse in Gilesgate, removing a large but decrepit Elizabethan merchant's house for the purpose; in 1973 the Council handsomely converted the warehouse into the town swimming baths. Bell's old tanneries on the Cockshaw side of Gilesgate were transformed by private enterprise into offices, workshops and homes which carefully preserved some visible relics of their smelly past. And the bandstand that Henry Bell had gifted to the town when the Abbey Grounds were thrown open as a public park in 1912 was refurbished, redecorated and revived as its surroundings were lavishly re-planned for the millennium.

Other developments, private and public, did much to enhance the quality of life in 20th-century Hexham. In particular, there was need to provide for fast expanding leisure needs. The moribund Queen's Hall, which had once been Town Hall and Corn Exchange and served at various times during the 20th century as ballroom, theatre, cinema and wartime emergency hospital, was rescued by joint action of the District and County Councils and brought back to life as a public library, arts centre and restaurant; the Queen's Hall became a major asset at the heart of voluntary and professional activities. The extensive Wentworth indoor and outdoor sports and leisure complex was developed alongside a car-park and supermarket where once there had been orchards. The town cinema began as the Gem in the first decade of the century, and survived (with some interruptions) into its last as the Forum. In a population somewhat overbalanced by the elderly who came to Hexham for an active retirement, voluntary societies, festivals and arts groups flourished.

Hexham in the late 20th century has added to its historic functions as market and administrative centre a newer role, as a pleasant place to visit or to live in. It is larger now, cleaner, more varied and more spacious than before, a thriving and attractive town. As Hexham approaches a new millennium it can look back on a long and exciting history, whose traces are preserved in the rich fabric of streets and buildings and open spaces, and in the time-honoured stones of the Archbishop's two towers and of the Abbey Church.

Some Books and Articles on the history of Hexham

Archaeologia Aeliana, published annually by the Society of Antiquaries of Newcastle upon Tyne, has occasional relevant and important articles; in recent years the most notable have been:
    Eric Cambridge et al, 'Hexham Abbey, a review of recent work' 5 XXIII 1995
    Stafford M Linsley 'Tyne Crossings at Hexham up to 1795' 5 XXII 1994
    Peter Ryder 'The Two Towers of Hexham' 5 XXII 1994

Tom Corfe (ed) *Before Wilfrid: Britons, Romans and Anglo-Saxons in Tynedale (Hexham Historian No 7)* HLHS 1997

The Hexham Historian, published annually by the Hexham Local History Society, with varied articles on the town's past and occasional special issues on single topics.

A B Hinds *Northumberland County History, Vol III, Hexhamshire, Part 1* Andrew Reid, Newcastle, 1896

C C Hodges *Ecclesia Hagustaldensis: the Abbey of St Andrew, Hexham* Privately published, 1888

C C Hodges and J Gibson *Hexham and its Abbey* Gibson, Hexham 1919

D P Kirby (ed) *Saint Wilfrid at Hexham* Oriel Press 1974

James Raine *The Priory of Hexham, its chronicles, endowments and annals* 2 vols, Surtees Soc 1864-5

A B Wright *An Essay towards a History of Hexham . . .* Davison, Alnwick 1823

Glovemaking became a major Hexham industry. With the Skinners, the Glovers formed one of the four Hexham guilds from Tudor times. By the 18th century the soft and supple 'Hexham tans' were widely known. In 1823 the first local historian, Andrew White, recorded some awesome statistics: 23,504 dozen pairs of gloves produced annually by a workforce of 1,000 sewing women working at home, with 110 men and boys as leather dressers and cutters. But foreign competition virtually killed the industry by mid century. Glovemaking has left few traces, though 'The Hexham Tans' is a popular modern restaurant.

INDEX

Illustrations are shown in **_bold italics_**

Abbey Church, Hexham (St Andrew's) 10, 11, 13, **_14, 15,_** 18, 25, 27, 32, 33, 34, 51, 57; arcades in, **_14,_** 15-16; beginnings of, 3, 6; building of, 15-16, 27; curates of, 32, 33, 34; font, 27; lecturers at, 32, 34; nave, **_10,_** 27, 34; organ, 28; paintings in, **_20,_** 27; as parish church, 15, 34; plans of, 10; Romanesque church, 15; screen, **_27;_** south transept, **_14,_** 16; see also Crypt, Frith Stool
Abbey Grounds **_35, 41, 50,_** 51, 57
Abbey, The (house) 34, 47
Acca, St 9, 11, 13; - Cross **_9_**
Acomb 40
Aelred of Rievaulx, St 14,18
Æthelthryth, Queen and St (Etheldreda) 3, 6
Ala Petriana 5
Alemouth road 38, 39, 40
Allgood family 36; Sir Lancelot, 36-37
Allendale 4, 13, 37
Alnmouth 40
Andrew, St 8, 9, **_20,_** 21, **_29;_** Church of, see Abbey Church; relics of, 9
Anglo-Saxons 3, 5, 6, 15
Annunciation (painting) **_20,_** 27
Armstrong Map **_44_**
Archbishop's Gaol **_22,_** 55
Augustine of Canterbury, St 9
Augustinians, see Canons, Augustinian

Back Street (St Mary's Chare) 17, **_35_**
Bailiff of Hexham 13, 16, 22, 24, 28
Baliol family 18, 21; John, 21
Bandstand **_41,_** 57
Bannockburn 21
Baptists 32
Battle Hill 25, **_48_**
Beaumont family 40, 47, 49; Wentworth Blackett, 51
Beaumont Street 47, **_48, 50_**
Beckensall, Stan (photographs by) **_14, 15, 19, 20, 26, 29_**
Bell, Henry **_56,_** 57
Benedict Biscop 6
Benson, Col 51
Berwick 21
Bishops 6, 7, 11
Bishop's Throne, see Frith Stool
Black Bull 37, 43, 48
Black Death 21
Blackett family 33, 34, 36; Sir Walter Calverley, 37, 39, 40, 43
Boards, Local 49, 51; elections for, 49; of Guardians, 49; of Health, 49, 51; School, 51
Borough 36, 54; - Book 36; - Court 17, 36, 47
Bridges, Hexham **_39, 40, 41,_** 43
Bronze Age 3

Bruce family 18, 21; Robert (Robert I) 21, 24, 25
Bucket, Hexham **_11_**
Bull Bank (Hallstile Bank) 37, **_48_**
Bywell 13, 24, 47

Cadwallon, King 5
Cambridge, Eric **_10_**
Campy Hill 16
canals 43
Canons, Augustinian 13-16,18, 21, 25, 27, 28
Carlisle 31, 32
Carnaby, Sir R 28, 34
Cathedra 11 (and see Frith Stool)
chantry chapels 27
chapels 47, **_48_**
chipboard 54
Chester-le-Street 12
Christianity 3, 5-6, 9, 13; Celtic vs Roman 6, 11
Churches, Nonconformist 32, 47
cinemas 57
Civic Society 55
coal 31, 39, 43
Coastley Row 18, 24
Cockshaw 16, **_17,_** 24, 32, 36; - Burn 2, 39
common keepers 36
Comyn, Richard 16, 18
constables 36
Cook, Anne 37
cookery books 37
Corbridge 3, **_4,_** 5, 6, 11, 21, 43
Crosses: Acca's **_9;_** Heavenfield 5-6; Market 35
Crypt, Saxon **_8, 9_**
Cuthbert, St 11, 12; Community of, 12

Dacre, Thomas Lord 28
David I King 18
David II King 24
Defoe, D 31
Dere Street 3
Denisesburn (Rowley Burn) 5-6
Derwentwater, Earl of 31
Devils Water **_4,_** 13, 24
Dilston 31
Dipton Woods 25, **_56_**
Dispensary 47
Dobson, John 51
Duke's House 44
Durham 3, **_4,_** 12, 16; Bishops of 12, 13

Eastwood Grange **_42_**
Ecgfrith, King 6
Edward I, King 21, 25
Edwin, King **_5_**
Eilaf, priest 13, 14, 15
Elizabeth, Queen 29, 31
Ely 6
Errington, Henry 43
Etheldreda, Queen, see Æthelthryth

False Jew 32
farming 18, 21-22, 24, 39
Fellside 51
Fenwick, Sir J 32, 34
ferryboats **_39,_** 40, 43
Fiennes, Celia 31, 34
First World War 53
Forster, Sir John 29, 32, 34
Four-and-Twenty 36
Frith Stool 6, 7, **_10,_** 11, 16
Flavinus, **_5_**
Flodden 28
Flood (1771) 43
fords 5, 16, **_39,_** 40, 43
fruit growing 39, 43-44, 53, 54

Gasworks 47
Gate, St Wilfrid's **_12,_** 14, 28
gatehouses **_12,_** 22, **_23,_** 24, 28
Gaul 5, 6
George & Dragon **_35,_** 36
Gibson, J P **_33, 45,_** 53
Gibson, W W 52, 53
Gilesgate (Gilligate) 14, 36, 43, **_56,_** 57
Glasse, Hannah 37
Glenwelt Road 40
glovemaking 2, 31, 54, **_58_**
Gott, William 40, 43
Grammar School 32, **_33,_** 36, 47 51
Gray and Collingwood, commissioners 28
green belt 53
guilds 36, 58

Hadrian's Wall 3, 4, 5, 39, **_41,_** 54, 55
Hagustald's Land 6, 12, 16
Halfdan, King 11
Hall, The (Bailiff's) 16, **_17,_** 22-24
Hallgate 24, 33, 51
Halliwell Dene 44
Hallstile Bank (Bull Bank) 24, 47
Haugh, The **_17_**
Haydon Bridge **_4_**
Heavenfield 5-6
Hebbron Chapel **_48_**
Hencotes 16, **_17,_** 36, 49
Henry VI, King 24
Henry VIII, King 28
Heron, John 28
Hextilda, 16, 18
Hexham, Battle of, 24, **_25;_**
Hexham, beginnings of, 3, 5, 16; burning of, 21; character of, 3, 34-35, 46, 51, **_54;_** growth, 53, 54; houses in 24, **_30,_** 34, 35, **_42,_** 53; manufactures in, 31, 46; Poor Law Union 49; population of, 44-46, **_47,_** 53; Roman site? 3-5; route centre 3, 43; setting of, 3, 31, 53; Station 43, **_46;_** topography 16, **_17;_** town 13, 16, 17, 18, 24, 34; town hall, 24, 35, 36, 51, 57; wards, 36; see also Abbey, Hall

59

Hexham Courant 49
Hexham Herald 49
Hexham Riot (1771) 36-38
Hexhamshire *4*, 6, 13, 16-17, 21, 24, 32, 33, 36, 51; - Common, *4*
Hoard, Hexham 11
Hodges, C C 2, *5, 10, 27, 55*
Holy Island 32; - House *34*, 35-36
Hospitals 14, 49, 56, 57
Hydro, The *56*

Industry, and industrial growth 31, 37, 39, 53
Inns 37
Inspeximus (1298) 25, 27
Iron Age 3

Jacobites 31-32, 36-37, 38
James VI and I, King 29
John of Beverley, St 11
John of Hexham, Prior 14
Johnson, W 43
justice 36, 38

Kingshaw Green 32

lead mining 37, 39, 43, 47, 54
Leschman, Prior Rowland *26*, 27, 28; chantry chapel of, *26*, 27; window of 28, *29*
Lindisfarne (Holy I) 6,11,12
Local Board of Health 49
Long Back Side 51

magistrates 36, 37-38
Malcolm III, King 13,18
Manor, Lord of the 32, 34, 36, 37, 47, 51; - courts, 36, 47; - Office 55
Margaret of Anjou, Queen 24-25
markets 3, 18, 28, 29, 31, 57
Market Cross 35
Market Place 16, *17*, 24, 27, *30*, 31, *32, 35*, 36, 37-38, *45*, 51
Market Steads 18, 36
Market Street 36
Mechanics' Institute 46, 47
Mercers Company 34
Methodists 47, *48*
Military Road 32, 40
Militia and Militia Riots 37-38
misericords *19*, 27
monastery 3, *5*
monks 14
Moore, Temple *10*
Moot Hall 16, 22, *23*, 24, 36
Morpeth 36, 37, 38
museums 55

Neolithic period 3
Nevilles Cross 24
Newcastle 31, 36
Newcastle to Carlisle Railway 43
Night Stair *15*, 16
Normans 12-13, 15, 18
North, The 28, 29, 31, 53
North, Roger 31
Northern Rebellion (1569) 29
North Tyne, River 3, *4*, 21, 43

Northumberland 31, 32, 38, *44;* County Council 51; Earls of, 18, 25, 28, 29
Northumbria, kingdom 3, 5-6, 11-12, 13, 18
North Yorks Militia 37

Ogle, Sir R 27
Orchard Place *42*
Oswald, St, King 5-6
Oswiu, King 6

pants 36, *45, 52*, 53, 55
Parker, Joseph 46
parks 51, 53, 57
Percy family 28, 29; and see Northumberland, Earls of
Peth Head 49, 53
Pilgrimage of Grace (1536) 28
place-names 6, 16
Poor Law 49
population 44-47, 53
Priest, hereditary 12, 13
Priestpopple 16, *17*, 36
Primitive Methodists 47, *48*
Priors, 22, 27, 34; Lodgings of, 28, *29*, 34
Priory, Hexham *12*, 14, 16, *17*, 18, 21, 24, 25, 28, 31; dissolution of, 28; - precinct wall, 14, 16, 17, *35, 36, 50;* properties of, *16*, 25, 27, 28
prisons 22, 55
Prospect House *5*, 16
Provosts 12
Public Health Act (1848) 49; - Report (1853) 49
Pulpitum 27

Quakers 32
Quatre Bras 40, 53
Queen Elizabeth High School 51, 55
Queen's Cave 25
Queen's Hall 57
querns 3

Railways 43, *46*, 53
Ramsay, T 32
Reformation 28
Regality 13, 18, 21, 28, 32, 36; and see Hexhamshire
Rheged 5, 6
Richard of Hexham, Prior 14, 16
Riot Act 38
Ritschel, George (senior and junior) 32
roads 3, 24, 31, 32, *38*, 39, 43; turnpikes and bars 40, 43, *44*
Roman Catholics 31, 32, 37, 47, 49, 51; mass houses and churches, 32, *34*, 47, *49*
Romans 3, 5, 6, 9, 11; standard-bearer *5*
Rome 6, 28
Rood Screen 27
Roses, Wars of 24
Rural District 17, 51, 54
Ryder, Peter *22, 23, 30*

St Andrew's Church, see Abbey
St Mary's Chapel (Church) 18, 24, *30*
St Mary's Chare *35*, 46, 47
St Mary's Church (RC) *49*, 51
St Oswald's Church 6
St Wilfrid's Gate *12*, 14, 28
sanctuary 16
scalerakers 36
schools 21, 32, 33, 47, 51
Scotland and Scots 3, *10*, 13, 18, 28, 36; invasions by, 21, 24, 25, 31
sculpture 9, *11, 26*, 27
Seal (Sele), The 6, *17*, 37, 40, 51
Sele School 51
Shambles 37
Shire Court 24
Skinners 2, 58; - Burn 24
Smeaton, John *39, 40, 43*
Smythson, Prior Thomas 28; Screen of, 27
Somerset, Duke of 24
South Tyne, River 3, 4
Stanegate 3
Steward, Manor 36, 47
Subscription School 47, 51
Swimming Baths *56*, 57

tanneries *2*, 24, 46, 54, 57
Temperley Fountain *52*, 53
Thompson, R 43
Thornton, Roger 27
Tillam, Thomas 32
Tourism *41, 54*
Tudors 28, 29
Tyne, River 3, *4*, 5, 6, 11, 13, 39; crossings of, *39*, 41, 43
Tynedale 3, 5, 13, 18, 21, 24, 32, 37, 39, 40, 43, 44; - District and Council, 54, 55, 57
Tyne Green *39*, 43
Tyneside 31, 39, 44

Uhtred, provost 13, 18
Umfraville family 13, 18
Urban District 17, 51, 54

vagrants 36
Vikings 11, 12

Wade, George 32, 37
Wallace, William 21, 25
Warden 16; - Hill 3
water supply 39, *45*, 49, *52*, 53
Wearmouth 6
Wentworth Centre 57
White, Andrew 58
Wilfrid, St, Bishop *1*, 2, 3, 6, *8*, 9, *10*, 11, 13, 18, *19*
William I, King 13
William III, King 32
Windmill Hill 3, 53
Wydon Burn Reservoir 49

Yarridge 16
York *12*, 1333; Archbishop of, 3, 6, 13, 16, 18, 21-22, 25, 27, 28, 32, 36, 57
Yorkshire 16, 18, 39